Effectively Steering the Ship

A CASE MANAGEMENT MANUAL FOR FAMILY LAW MEDIATORS

PAULA M. LAWHON

ABA
AMERICAN BAR ASSOCIATION
Dispute Resolution Section

Cover design by Elizabeth Kulak/ABA Design

Printed in the United States of America.

30 29 28 27 26   5 4 3 2 1

ISBN 978-1-63905-726-9

Contents

1

Introduction

A. The Need for Neutral Case Management: Someone to Steer the Ship

Family law cases are complex with many moving parts. There is an almost endless supply of factual and legal issues to unravel within the procedural framework of the court case. The emotional context varies significantly from case to case and frequently within each case. The adversarial case structure pits parties and professionals against each other, creating a competitive rivalry from the outset. Given these complexities and hurdles, family law cases can easily stagnate, and details can be overlooked, negatively impacting all aspects of the case.

An often-overlooked alternative to the traditional slog through endless discovery and courtroom battles is an experienced neutral case manager (i.e., a mediator with a specific focus on case management) to guide the parties and professionals more efficiently and collaboratively through the case. A case managing mediator serves as the team captain, drawing on their mediation and communication skills, legal knowledge, and organizational expertise to lead the parties and professionals through the various stages of the case. The neutral case manager guides the team from the outset to completion of the case and serves as the central information nexus for the case. Many mediators do not see themselves as case managers. And representing attorneys may not recognize the extent to which neutral mediators can support their case management needs.

While the benefits of neutral case management can apply to many areas of law, family law clients and professionals in particular seek more collaborative and client-centered dispute resolution processes, which a case managing mediator can provide. I hope this book will help family law mediators and attorneys recognize the important role the mediator can play in providing neutral case management in the form of centralization, structure, efficiency, and transparency throughout the case.

Most of us are aware of the inherent conflict of interest as legal professionals: Contentious cases that do not settle early in the case result in more hours to bill than less contentious cases. With that in mind, why should the family law professional seek centralization, efficiency, or collaboration in their cases? In other words, why should family law professionals care how or when a case is resolved if we all get paid regardless of when and how that happens?

As family law professionals, we should absolutely concern ourselves not only with our clients' financial interests, but also with their overall best interests and well-being. Protracted litigation negatively impacts the families we work with both financially and psychologically, which often leads to difficulties affecting health, work, parenting, and co-parenting. Prevailing research reminds us that high-conflict divorces are significantly more harmful to children throughout their lives than more collaborative divorces without ongoing conflict.[1] Not only does combative lawyering affect the families at the heart of these battles, but it also impacts the physical and mental health of professionals who operate on a daily basis in "white-collar combat zones." Armed with this knowledge, let's make the bold assumption as we work through this book that clients as well as family law professionals from all backgrounds are aligned with the goal of a smooth path toward resolution and finalization of each case.

Each case can be considered a metaphorical "ship" with plenty of stormy weather and unpredictable obstacles to push the ship off course and delay arrival at the desired destination. This book will provide practical guidance for the case managing family law mediator to effectively steer the ship through each stage of the case to guide the parties and professionals efficiently and collaboratively to the conclusion of the case.

My goal with this book is to provide a manual for family law mediators from every background to use and refer to based on the case management tools and examples provided throughout this book. These tools and the overall mediation style in this book are based on what has worked (and what has not worked) in my own mediation practice over the last 20 years. Along with my mediation partner, Shelley Kennedy, with whom I have worked for the last 15 years, we continuously build on and work to improve our case management procedures for the benefit of our clients. I hope that other family law professionals will use whatever tools or pointers in this book work for them, for the benefit of their own clients. However, the benefits of neutral case management are not limited to family law cases. The case management framework,

1. Cummings EM, Davies PT. *Marital Conflict and Children: An Emotional Security Perspective*. New York: Guilford Press; 2010:17–18.

considerations, and examples included can also be employed in nonfamily law cases, including elder care, probate, special education, and other complex areas where mediation benefits from strong coordination and a neutral at the center. Because these benefits extend to both the clients and the professionals, I encourage the liberal application of these tools to all practice areas.

B. The Civil Mediation Structure Is Insufficient in Family Law Cases

Family law mediations can differ significantly from the more traditional mediation structure found in many civil cases. Civil mediations (i.e., employment, real estate, personal injury, business disputes, etc.) typically involve one or two all-day intensive mediation sessions with each party and their counsel sequestered in separate rooms. After a long day of the mediator shuttling between the two rooms, everyone hopes to leave with a signed term sheet. The separate attorneys then work to draft the complete settlement agreement (hopefully without too many complications) to submit to the court to conclude the court case.

This traditional "one and done" settlement-conference-style mediation tends to employ a high-pressure clock-ticking strategy (as well as a steep daily rate for the mediator) that works well to encourage resolution in many civil mediations. This settlement-conference-style mediation can be useful in certain family law cases after much of the groundwork has been done by the separate attorneys to prepare the case for trial or mediation. However, when the groundwork to prepare the case is guided by an adversarial structure, the resulting dynamic of the clients and their counsel can be deleterious to productive settlement discussions in mediation. This can result in a contentious mediation that feels like a courtroom battle without a satisfactory outcome for anyone.

Family law cases also tend to be much more complex than standard civil cases. This is because the dissolution of a life together requires decisions to be made that impact every aspect of the parties' lives, often within the context of heightened emotions when the promise of a lifetime together is being dissolved. Such decisions impact homes, incomes, expenses, retirements, investments, short-term and long-term financial stability, and of course the children. Due to the unique context and breadth of issues to work through in family law cases, the traditional high-pressure civil mediation structure tends to fall short of meeting the needs of many divorcing couples.

In my experience, the ideal managed family law mediation format includes frequent meetings spread out over several months throughout the case, depending on the preferred pace and availability of the parties and the professionals. My preferred cadence is to meet every two to three weeks for one to four hours in each meeting. I have found that this structure and pace allow for critical case management to take place during the case initiation, information gathering, and financial disclosure stages as well as the stages of settlement negotiations before formalizing agreements and finalizing the court case. And while family law cases are not known for such linearity, having a neutral professional manage each of these fluid stages from a unified and neutral perspective tends to keep the case on track with everyone working as a team toward common goals. While the pace of meeting every two to three weeks may not be realistic or needed in every case, having a default pace provides structure and builds on momentum and ensures there are no unnecessary delays in keeping the case progressing forward toward resolution.

With this structure, the neutral family law mediator can take on a much more central role from the outset of the case through entry of final judgment than is possible with the typical settlement-conference-style mediation structure. This ongoing neutral case management role provides benefits to the parties and the professionals throughout the case to move the case forward more efficiently and collaboratively to final judgment. For families seeking a more amicable and efficient process than what the traditional divorce offers, a neutral case managing mediator can help meet those goals by serving as the neutral guide to the parties and counsel through each stage of the case.

Family law attorneys are aware of the vast number of factual and legal issues that may arise in each case. We are trained to identify issues that need to be addressed in court or in settlement discussions. And we learn to effectively argue those issues and prepare motions, stipulations, and settlement agreements as trial attorneys. While such training does not typically focus on case management skills, experienced attorneys tend to develop their own methods of moving a case through the various stages and toward resolution. The problem with the default model of moving a case toward resolution is there are two attorneys—one for each party—who are working within an adversarial court structure on opposing sides even outside of court. The adversaries often fight each other from the initiation of the case, through discovery, through each of the issues to be resolved, all the way until the court case is eventually finalized via settlement negotiations or trial. Cohesive case management can be difficult, if not impossible, in such cases. What results is often protracted and expensive litigation, which could have been avoided with a more unified case structure provided by a neutral case manager.

Unlike separate attorneys, who have an individual client and responsibility in each case, the neutral family law mediator works for both parties. The mediator is ideally situated to closely manage the parties through each stage in these emotionally, factually, and legally complex cases. And the mediator is well positioned to serve as the central hub of information and case management to benefit the parties and the professionals. As the central information nexus, the neutral mediator can track the details of the case and each tentative agreement without risk that an assumption might be made in favor of one party over the other.

The unique responsibility of the neutral mediator to both parties, in addition to the parties' access to the private mediator for more frequent meetings, can allow for a more organized and streamlined passage through the complexities of each case, as detailed throughout this book.

C. Who Needs This Book?

This book is written for all family law professionals including attorney–mediators, non-attorney mediators, family law attorneys, and law students considering a career in family law mediation. While this book is written from the perspective of a family law attorney–mediator, the goal of this book is to guide all family law professionals working as neutrals engaged by both parties to help reach a mediated settlement without litigation, including attorneys and non-attorneys.

Non-attorney mediators include mediators with therapy backgrounds, finance backgrounds, coaching backgrounds, and other dispute resolution backgrounds. Such mediators can serve in the same central case manager role as attorney–mediators, though some adjustments will be needed in drafting formal agreements and filing pleadings on behalf of both parties. That said, some jurisdictions do not permit attorney–mediators or non-attorney mediators to draft formal agreements; instead the neutral mediator prepares term sheets or a Memorandum of Understanding (MOU) for separate representing attorneys to then draft the legally enforceable agreements. It is therefore critical for mediators of all backgrounds to know the requirements of their local jurisdictions. This includes requirements related to mediation, rules of confidentiality, and formalization of agreements, as well as court filing requirements, so each mediator can best support the clients who look to them for guidance through this process.

The primary purpose of this book is to encourage and support other family law mediators (including those considering a transition to mediation) to become more comfortable in their roles as case managers to guide mediation clients and counsel more effectively through the process to a successful conclusion. This book is also intended to encourage separate family law attorneys to make room for and rely on the mediators in their cases as the central information and case management hub. Mediators taking on the role of case manager in any complex case can benefit the parties as well as the professionals by paving the path for a smoother, more productive and efficient case resolution, which translates to happy clients.

Although my family law mediation practice is based in the San Francisco Bay Area in Marin County, California, the case management needs outlined in this book are applicable to family law cases throughout the country (and beyond!). This is because the core substantive issues of family law—asset division, child custody, and support—are present in every jurisdiction, regardless of differences in the laws applicable to those core substantive issues. Although procedures and terminology vary by jurisdiction, the basic approach to managing cases, clients, issues, and professionals is applicable to family law mediators everywhere.

In this book, I will discuss the ways in which attorneys and non-attorneys become mediators and the skills and qualities needed to be a successful family law mediator. I will identify the substantive and procedural areas of family law cases that can benefit from neutral case management. And I will provide practical guidance for both experienced and newer mediators to improve their case management skills at each stage of the case.

My hope with this book is that other family law mediators, as well as mediators in fields outside of mediation, will become great case managers so they can develop full and rewarding mediation practices focused on case management and successful outcomes for the parties and the professionals involved. An all-around win!

2

The Pieces of the Family Law Case Puzzle

Each family law case is made up of various and unique pieces that all need to come together into something like a completed puzzle. The finished puzzle is based on the individual clients and their financial and relationship history, which determines the specific legal and factual issues to be resolved, as well as the professionals engaged as the clients' separate or joint advisors. This is why no two cases are ever identical in their issues or outcomes.

A. Types of Cases and Issues Encountered by the Mediator

There are numerous types of family law cases, including dissolutions of marriage and registered domestic partnerships, legal separations, annulments, custody cases, parentage cases, child support cases, guardianships, and adoptions. For purposes of this book, we will use the dissolution of marriages or registered domestic partnerships (collectively "divorce") as the default case type since divorce is the most complete family law case, often incorporating elements of the other case types.

Each divorce case may include any combination of substantive issues, including child custody, child support, spousal support, division of simple or complex assets and liabilities, tax filing and apportionment of tax liability, health and life insurance, and reimbursements. Each individual substantive issue may include numerous sub-issues to unravel, which can look vastly different from one case to the next.

The division of assets and liabilities might include personal and commercial real estate; vesting employer equity in private or publicly held companies; vesting private equity and venture capital interests, privately held businesses, and other private or public investments; retirement accounts and pension plans; as well as personal property, family heirlooms, and intellectual property. These assets may be located out of state or abroad with unique sets of applicable rules, laws, and tax issues. There may be issues of transmutations, commingling of marital and separate assets, misuse of marital funds, and other breaches of fiduciary duties, all of which can impact the division of the estate. There may also be premarital agreements or postmarital agreements, inheritances and other sources of separate property, estate planning, life insurance, and expenses for adult children.

Support is another area with an extraordinary number of issues, perspectives, and potential outcomes. Many cases require the mediator, the parties, and the other professionals to build a unique spousal support (aka alimony) and expense-sharing structure. This often needs to happen within the context of strong emotional or philosophical differences about the concept of spousal support in addition to the parties' specific factual and financial history. And while all U.S. states have their own guidelines for calculating child support,[1] there are still many cases in which an alternative structure is desired or needed. This includes cases in which a parent's complex compensation structure does not fit neatly into the traditional child support structure to meet the needs of the children, cases in which a parent's extraordinarily high income warrants a deviation from guideline child support, or other situations in which the legal framework is not ideal for the family's circumstances.

While the financial issues in each case are numerous, there can be countless issues to resolve regarding parenting (i.e., child custody). Parenting issues may include a default weekly schedule, holiday schedule, agreements regarding travel, communication, introduction of new partners, and decision-making on everything from health, school, religion, and extracurricular activities to piercings, tattoos, and issues of health and safety with each parent. While custody issues are often addressed in mediation along with the financial issues, a parenting expert may be engaged (see Section C, The Professionals in the Case, later in this chapter) to work on more in-depth parenting issues, which may include creating a formal co-parenting plan. This division into financial/legal mediation and separate parenting mediation can work well in cases in which ongoing parenting issues threaten to eclipse progress on the financial and legal mediation or when additional parenting support could benefit the family. There is also an integrative option of co-mediation, in which both professionals work together as a team with the parties in mediation sessions, which can be a very supportive structure for many families.

These substantive areas and each of the related sub-issues are the core puzzle pieces that need to be identified at the outset of the case and which will eventually come together to create a unique and cohesive settlement structure

1. Justia, "Child Support Laws and Forms: 50-State Survey" (2023).

in each individual case. As mediators, we cannot know what obstacles we might face or which areas might include smooth sailing or rough seas, and we must be prepared for anything and everything to help the families who have come to us for guidance.

B. The Heart of the Family Law Case

At the heart of every case are the individuals whose marriage is being legally dissolved and whose financial relationship is ending or changing in cases with children or other ongoing issues. Every aspect of the clients' personalities, relationship, and separation can influence how the divorce proceeds. This can include each client's personality type, their relationship history, how and why they separated, how they have treated each other during separation, and their individual relationships with their children. Each of these factors can determine whether their path in divorce will be positive and collaborative or whether it will be fraught with challenges at every turn. The mediator can work to understand the parties' dynamic and their individual needs to inform the mediator's approach in their role as case manager.

Other aspects of their relationship will be relevant to the mediation as well. The individuals in each case may have had a short-term or long-term marriage or may have cohabited prior to legalizing their union. Either of the parties may have mental health issues or a history of substance abuse and may benefit from having complementary mental health or sobriety professionals involved. There may be minor or young adult children with financial and nonfinancial issues to resolve. Their children may have special needs that presented prior to the separation or may need specific support now due to the changes the family is undergoing. The parties may have a more traditional or nontraditional relationship. One party may be a numbers person while the other is not. One party may be assertive or a quick decision maker while the other may be more easygoing or anxious or need more time to process information and explore all options before feeling comfortable with any decision. Each of these factors can influence the tone and trajectory of the case as well as the mediator's approach and communication with the parties throughout the case.

Other interpersonal dynamics or events can impact how smooth the divorce process will be or how the mediator approaches communication with the parties. This can include how the couple managed finances during their relationship. Did they have joint or separate finances? Was there open communication about finances or limited financial transparency during the marriage? Was there a financial or fiduciary breach such as the discovery of extensive debt, hidden assets, or unilateral spending down of shared assets? There can also be emotional breaches, which can encompass anything from emotional or physical abuse to infidelity, including individual or multiple intimate relationships, engaging with sex workers, or even extensive and expensive use of pornography. Any of these breaches can significantly impact the final outcome of the case as well as the divorce process itself.

Some clients may avoid discussing reasons for the divorce given the complexities of "fault" in the decline of a relationship. Such topics, if they are addressed in mediation, can more safely be discussed in separate meetings with each client so the mediator can understand each party's experience or concerns. Of course, some mediators only meet jointly with the parties, considering separate meetings to be impermissible ex parte communications, while other mediators' practices exclusively involve separate caucuses. While my own preference is for each meeting to be held jointly, I will schedule separate sessions before joint meetings to establish rapport and gather insight into these types of interpersonal issues and each party's needs and concerns when I think that might benefit the mediation.

In addition to the family dynamics, there are countless ways the decision to divorce may have occurred. Any number of events or traumatic experiences may have led to the divorce or may have occurred since separation, which will all impact the divorce. The divorcing couple may have arrived jointly at the decision to separate and remain friendly and respectful despite the difficult circumstances. Or the decision to divorce may have been made unilaterally or abruptly, with one partner still in shock after years or decades of marriage. How that decision was reached and communicated between the couple is just as important as what steps they may or may not have taken to process the emotional issues surrounding the end of their marriage. Each of these factors can significantly impact what the path to a final divorce judgment looks like for each couple.

When one spouse experiences a perceived trauma or disrespect from the other spouse outside of the mediation, this can lead to devolving communication and good will. It can be difficult for a spouse to dig deep into their reserves of patience and magnanimity in settlement discussions when the intensity of their pain or anger drives them in the opposite direction.

Even couples who have thoughtfully discussed and planned their separation together can negatively impact their divorce process with the introduction of new relationships before expectations can be set around this topic. Many newly separated individuals in this situation are surprised by the effect that "premature dating" can have on the outcome and timing of their divorce. This is exacerbated when serious relationships just after separation involve someone known to the other spouse, such as a parent of their child's classmate or a teacher. Actions that erode the remaining good will between the parties can make it harder to bring compassion, empathy, and generosity into the settlement discussion, which can be important in finding paths to settlement.

Ideally, both parties will have worked through emotionally processing the end of the marriage prior to starting their divorce. Couples who engage in joint or individual counseling prior to starting their divorce are often more emotionally ready to tackle the divorce process and the decisions that need to be made. Such couples can work together to unravel and understand the reasons for the separation and set goals for how they wish to proceed in their divorce, creating a smoother path in the divorce process. For divorcing parents, this often means taking the time to identify shared goals for the divorce and discussing expectations about communication with the children about the separation and living arrangements. When potentially sensitive issues (such as timing for introducing the children to new partners) are discussed up front, both partners know what to expect, which supports productive communication in and outside of the mediation.

If there has not been end-of-relationship emotional processing prior to starting the divorce process, the parties may be in such different mental states that it may be challenging to productively communicate, even with an experienced mediator. For example, if one spouse is reeling from a (seemingly) abrupt ending of the relationship, it can be difficult for that spouse to move through all the significant decisions that need to be made in a divorce. If one spouse is resisting the divorce, they may consciously or unconsciously delay various stages of the case, which can cause confusion or frustration for the other party as well as the professionals.

As family law professionals, we want our clients to be able to easily access the part of their brains needed for rational executive decision making (i.e., the prefrontal cortex). By the time they are working with us, we want clients to be past the "fight-flight-freeze" fear-response mode known in neuroscience and psychology as the activation of the sympathetic nervous system. These protective fear responses are particularly useful in short-term emergency situations. They are not so helpful in making thoughtful and rational decisions impacting children, homes, immediate and long-term financial planning, and all the other significant life decisions that need to be made in a divorce.

There may be occasions in which the mediator observes in potential clients that it may be premature to start mediation when the separation or a traumatic revelation has just occurred weeks prior. In such cases, the emotional wounds are still raw and there is an emotional unwinding that needs to happen before both parties are truly ready to engage in productive discussions in mediation. Occasionally one party will be eager to get started while the other party still appears shell-shocked. The initiating party may feel they have been waiting to get started for months or even years. Meanwhile, the other party is trying to catch up emotionally and get their bearings as to all the changes they are facing and can feel frozen in their processing and decision-making abilities. While many individuals in these circumstances are reluctant to engage in marriage counseling, I still encourage meeting with an experienced marriage counselor to discuss and process the emotional dissolution of the relationship. Taking this step can set both clients up for a productive mediation when they are both ready to move forward with their divorce.

Ultimately, the individuals at the heart of the case are the decision makers, whether the issues are mediated or litigated. This is because even in litigated cases, the parties decide what issues are litigated and what issues are resolved via direct discussions between the parties, with the help of the professionals, or through court-based settlement conferences before trial. In mediation, the mediator is there to help the parties reach decisions together by providing a structure, an open line of communication, options and alternatives, and legal and factual bases for considering proposals. Ideally, the mediator will also be able to provide the neutral case management described in this book to help shepherd the parties through each of the stages of the case and set the parties up for a successful mediation.

C. The Professionals in the Case

The divorcing couple may choose to rely on any number of professionals to help them through the transition of separation and through the divorce process. Just as the specific substantive and emotional issues in each case vary widely, the number and type of professionals can also differ significantly from one case to the next. These include financial professionals, mental health and parenting professionals, and legal professionals.

1. Financial Professionals

The various financial experts involved in a case might include joint or separate forensic accountants or financial advisors, including certified divorce financial analysts (CDFAs), certified financial planners (CFPs), and wealth advisors. These financial experts may be directly involved throughout the case or may be consulted for limited issues either as joint or separate consultants.

Other financial experts with a more specific focus may be consulted by one party or their attorney or by both parties as a joint neutral expert. This can include real estate brokers, mortgage brokers, and health and life insurance brokers; disability benefits experts, retirement experts, and business valuation experts; and appraisers of residential or commercial real estate, artwork, and other collections.

Setting expectations regarding the work of the financial professionals is a critical step at the outset of each case. Raising the option of engaging a neutral financial professional can often circumvent one party attorney hiring a separate forensic accountant and assuming the other party will also hire their own, leading to a more time-consuming, costly, and adversarial process.

The first step is to identify and agree on the scope of issues requiring a financial professional in the case. As soon as the issue of engaging a financial professional is raised, the mediator should discuss with the parties or professionals whether there are benefits to having the work conducted by a neutral professional rather than two separate financial professionals.

If there is consensus for a joint expert, there can then be a discussion of options for professionals to fill the role, including which credentials are appropriate (e.g., CDFA, forensic accountant, business valuation expert, or real estate appraiser). Then the mediator and professionals can suggest and discuss the specific professionals who might be a good fit for the case. The allocation of fees for the financial professionals, whether joint or separate, should also be discussed at this time. Once everyone has agreed, the mediator can contact the neutral professional(s), outline the scope of work, determine their availability and fees, coordinate the engagement process, and set up the initial meeting with the financial professional to get them on board.

In cases in which the mediator is engaged after the separate legal and financial teams are already assembled, the mediator might meet with each team separately or with both teams jointly to understand the scope of the financial issues and the status of their work, and determine the next steps in the case.

2. Mental Health and Parenting Professionals

Mental health and parenting professionals are often involved in family law cases in various roles. Child therapists, individual therapists for each party, marriage counselors, or family therapists who work with multiple family members may continue or start working with a family during the divorce process.

There may also be one or more parenting professionals involved in a case in any of the following roles:

- Co-parent counselors are jointly engaged therapists who specialize in child custody mediation. They help the parents create a formal co-parenting plan and provide ongoing support as needed. There are also custody mediation attorneys with particular expertise in custody litigation matters as well as court-based mediators with mental health backgrounds, which we collectively consider custody mediators. Private custody mediators can also serve as co-mediators with a legal/financial mediator, with each professional taking responsibility for the issues within their respective scopes of expertise to contain the issues and personalities and provide the level of support that is needed in certain cases.
- Parenting coaches are engaged in various roles, typically working for one parent rather than for both. Some coaches help parents improve the health and safety of the parenting or home environment; such coaches provide real-time guidance during or outside of parenting visits, which can be helpful when a parent is stepping into a new role or getting used to a two-household family structure. Other parenting coaches provide support to one parent engaged in mediation or a formal collaborative dispute resolution process; each parent has their own parenting coach with the goal of ensuring a child-centered approach and outcome on the parenting issues in the case, with the two parenting coaches speaking to collateral sources when needed and working together to resolve the parents' custody disagreements.
- Parenting coordinators (PCs) or "special masters" are experienced custody/parenting attorneys or mental health professionals who have been appointed by stipulation and order to make binding decisions on specific parenting issues. PCs are typically engaged in higher conflict cases in which more immediate and ongoing tiebreaking is needed regarding all manner of parenting issues. The PC's scope of authority is limited to not overstep the court's authority to make more significant decisions on legal or physical custody or other substantial changes to the time-share allocation. Some PCs help parents communicate and make day-to-day decisions, only ruling when the parents cannot agree. Other cases involve a two-tiered mediation/PC process in which the parents are the decision makers within the mediation with a separate decision making PC in place as backup when a decision or order is needed.

- Custody evaluators are formally appointed to interview children and parents, gather information from other sources like schools or child-care providers, and make recommendations to the court or to the PC and parents. Custody evaluators can be ordered by the court but can also be agreed to by the parents via stipulation and order when an evaluation (limited or otherwise) would be useful for the parents to reach parenting agreements together without the court's involvement. Occasionally, appointing a custody evaluator by agreement can be a useful tool in mediation as well.

The family law mediator can help keep track of the various parenting professionals and their roles. This may include making referrals and introductions, identifying each professional's role, working on stipulations for appointment, and coordinating meetings of the various professionals when needed. However, given their mental health and family systems expertise, it can be even more beneficial for custody mediators to take responsibility for coordinating meetings of the mental health and parenting professionals, including checking in with each of the professionals directly and reporting back to the group.

Communication between neutral professionals is beneficial for the mediation process. The custody mediator should be encouraged to keep the financial/legal mediator updated via short summaries or copying the financial/legal mediator on all correspondence, and the financial/legal mediator should do the same with the custody mediator, establishing an agreed-upon system that works in each individual case. In co-mediation cases, both mediators copy each other on all correspondence so there are no information gaps between the co-mediators, since this shared communication is one of the benefits of co-mediation.

In certain cases, there are no parenting professionals involved, and the mediator (attorney or non-attorney) works directly with clients to create their parenting agreements. In my own practice, we mediate parenting issues as part of the overall divorce mediation unless the need for a parenting expert presents itself. Parenting issues include custody, time share, holidays, vacations, and decision making. The custody issues we mediate without a parenting expert tend to involve lower levels of conflict and higher levels of cooperation between the parents who are jointly seeking neutral guidance. For cases in which more substantial parenting guidance or ongoing support is needed, we recommend a co-parent counselor to work directly with the parties or to work within the mediation as a co-mediating neutral.

3. Legal Professionals

Other than mediators, the professionals most frequently involved in any given case are each client's separate family law attorneys. Separate attorneys may be involved in the background as consulting counsel or in the forefront as representing counsel (i.e., attorneys of record with the court). Clients with consulting attorneys are considered pro per or pro se (i.e., self-represented) litigants from the perspective of the court, because the mediator does not represent either or both parties in their court case even if the mediator is an attorney.

The mediator and any separate attorneys in each case should establish an agreed communication protocol at the outset of their involvement. Such protocols include whether the mediator will copy attorneys on all emails or only direct correspondence to the clients who can then decide what to share with their separate attorneys. This can also include whether the attorneys are comfortable with both parties and counsel included in some or all email discussions (i.e., as a limited waiver of the rules of professional conduct, which prohibit an attorney for one party communicating directly with another represented party). While some litigation-focused attorneys may not permit full-group correspondence (other than from the neutral mediator), "mediation-friendly" attorneys tend to recognize the efficiency and productivity of full-group emails, particularly on scheduling or case management emails, and trust the mediator to manage the flow of information.

Family law attorneys are not the only legal professionals involved in a family law case. Trust and estate attorneys, tax attorneys, bankruptcy attorneys, corporate or business attorneys, real estate attorneys, elder and disability attorneys, or immigration attorneys may be involved directly or indirectly in any case. The neutral mediator may interact directly with these attorneys as joint consultants by initiating the engagement of the professionals, outlining specific questions to be answered for the group or the parties, or discussing the issues directly with the legal professional and reporting back to the group. For example, the parties might introduce the mediator to their personal tax accountant to clarify the parties' questions on the advantages and disadvantages of joint or separate personal tax filings and allocation of liability for certain tax years. In other situations, each party or their family law counsel may communicate directly with their own separately engaged consultants such as a tax accountant or attorney, bankruptcy attorney, or trusts and estate attorney and report back to the group as needed.

And in some cases, there are no other attorneys. These cases just involve the two parties and the mediator working together from the start to the finish of the case. In such cases, the parties are considered self-represented, because the mediator does not represent either party but is instead their neutral guide through the case. The percentage of mediations in our office without separate consulting or representing attorneys varies but is typically around 30–40 percent of our caseload at any time. These cases also tend to involve lower conflict and higher levels of trust between the parties, though not all cases without separate attorneys are smooth sailing from start to finish. There are some cases in which the parties are amicable in one meeting and in the next meeting the winds have shifted like a sudden storm. This can happen regardless of other professionals' involvement. The mediator can work to determine the underlying source of the conflict to help get the parties back on track toward productive settlement discussions.

There are also cases in which the parties are working together in mediation without separate counsel until one party indicates their desire to consult with separate counsel or requests to bring their counsel into the mediation. Or the mediator might recommend consultation with separate counsel on a certain issue or in a certain situation. The other party may prefer no counsel involvement or prefer to keep consulting attorneys in the distant background. The mediator, always prepared for anything, must adapt to work with the new dynamic that has presented itself since one of the parties has identified a specific need regarding their legal counsel and can typically be supported in such a request. The mediator can help identify the reasons for the change and help both parties understand the revised structure or other options that may work better for their situation.

D. A Successful Outcome Is in the Eye of the Beholders

Throughout this book, "successful outcomes" generally refers to the final judgment of dissolution in a case. However, mediators should not make assumptions as to which direction any case might take or how it will conclude. While the mediator guides and structures the process, the needs, interests, and decisions of the parties themselves drive and determine their own outcome.

I encourage all parties to approach their cases without assumptions about what shape their final settlements might ultimately take and to instead maintain an open mind to settlement options they might not have considered yet. Our goal as mediators is to balance the needs and interests of *both* parties in crafting the best possible settlement, not just the structure one party may want or feel is the only "fair" outcome. I frequently remind clients in various ways that I do not have a predetermined outcome for their case, even though I know the law and the facts of their case, because those are not the only things that determine the outcome. I might even say something like the following when needed: "I come into each case with an open mind and need you to do the same in order for mediation to work. Do you both think you can do that?"

It is also worth noting that a final judgment is not the only successful outcome, even for a case that starts out as a divorce. A case that starts out as a divorce may pivot to a temporary separation, a legal separation, or a reconciliation with or without a postmarital agreement. A postmarital mediation may pivot to reconciliation without a written agreement, or to a divorce. The mediator can pivot with the parties to support and guide their journey wherever it may lead and provide options and a forum for openly discussing these issues and problem solving together. The mediator can be a fluid guide, navigating even when the mediation takes an unexpected turn or a new course entirely.

Most long-time mediators have had the experience of meeting with couples who have decided to divorce, only for the mediator to sense ambivalence about the divorce from both parties. In those situations, the mediator can bring a respectful curiosity to the discussion to find out more about what led to the decision to divorce and uncover what is at the heart of the perceived ambivalence. Sometimes it's not what the clients are saying but what they aren't saying, or it may be a repeated feeling the mediator has, even if they can't determine the source. In such situations, the mediator may want to pause to identify the feeling or what triggered it.

Taking cues from the content and emotionality by one or both parties, the mediator might say something with a gentle opening such as: "I know it is hard to be here, and I wonder if we want to take a couple minutes to talk about what's going on for both of you." Or something more direct when the signs of ambivalence are more obvious: "Taking this step toward divorce can be really difficult—would you like to talk about whether this is the right path for the two of you?" Or: "I can see how much you both care about each other and how difficult this is. I often meet with couples in your same situation when there is still a question about whether to keep working on the marriage or to take steps toward divorce. If we want to get into the issues you are trying to solve in more detail, we might be able to explore whether there are other options that could work better for you than a divorce."

The experienced family law mediator will be able to discuss alternatives to divorce mediation, including marital mediation,[2] discernment counseling,[3] or even a new couples counselor, as well as various alternative legal options, such as informal separations, legal separations, and postmarital agreements. Mediations that start as divorces and end up as postmarital agreements can be transformative for the parties and rewarding for the mediator. These outcomes could be vastly different if a rigid mediation process stuffs each set of clients into a box and sends them down the divorce chute without exploring what is happening in the room and what the clients actually need.

When it is clear that options other than divorce could meet the needs of the parties, the mediator could say something like the following: "The more I know about the two of you and your 'real life' goals, the more I can help you explore options and address the concerns you each have, whatever it ends up looking like at the end." Or this: "There might be other options that might work better for both of you than divorce if you want to discuss other solutions. We can structure the legal part around what you are actually trying to do, so maybe we can start with what you want as a couple or as individuals and not start with the assumption we are going down the divorce path."

If the mediator feels the parties are not ready for divorce mediation or could benefit from an alternative structure (e.g., co-mediation, or starting out in co-parent counseling before starting the financial/legal mediation, or even heading straight to court), the mediator should discuss their observations with the parties, even if that ultimately means losing them as mediation clients. The mediator's focus on helping the parties whatever their needs may be—without self-interest by the mediator—strengthens the parties' confidence in the mediator as a trusted guide in an area in which both parties typically have little to no experience. When both parties trust they are in good hands with their mediator, that translates to trust in the mediator and in the mediation process itself. That trust can reduce anxiety and promote productive communication and needs-based discussions throughout the mediation. Many such

2. Marital mediation, distinct from divorce mediation or couples counseling, is a process in which a mediator works with the couple to address areas of friction, improve communication, and help make decisions and reach agreements together for the benefit of the marriage. Marital mediation does not replace couples therapy, but can be a complementary modality to improve the marriage and avoid divorce.

3. Discernment counseling is a short-term focused therapy for couples who may be on the brink of divorce and need guidance on whether to work on the marriage or proceed with divorce.

clients have referred their friends and family to our office even though I didn't ultimately work with the referring parties, because I recognized they needed to be somewhere else and made the introduction to pave their better path forward.

The reward to the mediator is not always in helping clients to reach substantive agreements and resolve their cases. With an open mind, there can be tremendous satisfaction to the mediator in knowing the parties were able to get to exactly where they needed to be, and might not have found that place without insight and guidance from their trusted mediator.

3

What Exactly Is Case Management?

In my family law mediation practice, we consider case management to be just as important as helping the parties reach agreements in mediation sessions. Since the focus of this book is to highlight the importance of case management in family law cases and help mediators learn how to provide neutral case management, let's examine what "case management" means in the context of family law cases and what the role of the case managing mediator can be.

From a high-level metaphorical perspective, managing the case means steering the ship, passengers, and crew toward the passengers' desired destination via the most efficient course, away from rougher seas, with the goal of minimizing infighting among passengers and among crew (or mutinying!), without anyone falling overboard or the ship capsizing or crashing. The farther we carry this metaphor, the more fitting it is to what can happen in a family law case.

A. The Importance of Case Management in Family Law Mediations

Metaphors aside, from a practical day-to-day working perspective for the mediator, the case management needed in family law mediations includes any or all of the following:

- Guiding the parties and any separate or joint professionals through each of the stages of the case from the initiation of the court case through entry of final judgment.
- Taking responsibility for each of the necessary procedural steps in every stage of the case or agreeing on a plan for who will be responsible for each step.
- Helping the parties and counsel identify the specific settlement issues in the case.

- Creating a plan with the parties and professionals for obtaining and sharing all information necessary for the parties to be able to make decisions, including financial disclosures and any other informal discovery, or outside information.
- Coordinating the engagement of any neutral experts and the scope of work needed and managing the flow of information to and from the neutral experts.
- Determining the best structure for communicating with the clients and professionals in and outside of mediation sessions, for sharing information and documents, and for scheduling meetings.
- Facilitating settlement discussions in mediation sessions and separate meetings, including structuring the meetings as joint or separate or a combination of both.
- Tracking settlement terms, open issues, and action items and sharing this information with the parties, including bullet point summaries, term sheets, and financial calculations and spreadsheets.
- Keeping all parties and professionals on course by setting and managing timelines and scheduling follow-up meetings.
- Drafting formal agreements, including any temporary or interim agreements as well as the final settlement agreement.
- Tracking and managing proposed edits and various versions of the formal agreements and scheduling mediations or case management meetings to discuss issues that may arise in the formalization stage.
- Coordinating the signing of formal agreements and judgment documents required by the court.
- Submitting the signed settlement agreement and judgment documents required to obtain the final divorce judgment from the court.
- Providing signed agreements and court orders to the parties and professionals.
- Managing any transactions triggered by the settlement agreement, including any settlement payments, retirement transfers, equity and other account transfers, real estate transfers, vehicle transfers, or estate planning and corporate updates, and tying up any other loose ends.
- Mediating any postjudgment settlement issues that may arise in the future, including income and support reconciliations, parenting agreement modifications, and other amendments to the settlement agreement.

B. Identifying and Organizing All Those Details

To manage each of the steps involved in the various stages of the case, it is critical to identify and organize all the details from a neutral perspective throughout the mediation process. From the start of the case through entry of final judgment, the mediator needs to remember that "the devil is in the details." Devilish details, including assumptions or unanswered questions, can derail a settlement if not addressed and resolved before getting to the stage of drafting formal agreements.

In organizing and managing case details and tentative agreements, the mediator should never make assumptions that could advantage one party over the other. For example, if one party agrees to pay the initial mediation retainer, the mediator can include that detail in the follow-up summary and also flag the related questions to be discussed, including whether this was an advance to be reallocated and reimbursed or whether there is an agreement for one party to take responsibility for all mediation fees or just the initial retainer. The mediator can also note that the allocation of separate attorneys' fees or other professionals' fees still needs to be discussed. While some clients discuss and resolve these fee issues prior to starting mediation and have the same understanding, in other cases, there are only partial conversations with different assumptions made by the clients, which the mediator can work to understand and resolve when needed.

Flagging these issues in written summaries with "TBDs" for "to be determined" can be broad, such as: "Susan paid the initial retainer deposit. *TBD how mediation fees are being paid overall and *TBD how your separate attorneys' fees are being paid." This highlights that there are details to confirm since one or both parties or counsel may have some assumptions about what that initial payment means and noting this allows for a complete discussion on options and agreements.

When separate counsel are involved in coordinating the payment of the initial mediation deposit or payment, they know to make it clear whether such payment is an advance subject to reallocation or reimbursement or whether one party has agreed to take sole responsibility for the neutral mediation fees. However, individual clients are not typically as familiar with these nuances, and the mediator will need to discuss their intentions and agreements without assuming there is an agreement on anything other than exactly what was communicated to the mediator.

Keep in mind that just raising the related issues may result in frustration for the party who assumed all fee issues were already resolved, but could result in relief for the other party who didn't think the related issues were even discussed, much less resolved, and appreciates the opportunity to have the conversation in mediation. As the neutral guide, the mediator can help the parties navigate their different assumptions with patience and clarity and without judgment.

Listening carefully and identifying the nuances of what is and is not being communicated is critical to the mediator's work. Identifying and organizing these details in a neutral manner, without assumptions and with an eye toward the details that will be included in the formal agreements, builds trust for the parties and counsel to know the mediator is tracking all issues and updates in a neutral manner and following up on all open questions, regardless of whether that benefits one party or the other. Tracking and resolving all open questions throughout the case ensures there are no surprises for the parties or their counsel when the final settlement agreement is drafted. This upfront and ongoing organizing and tracking helps guide the case toward final resolution with fewer surprises and a smoother and therefore more efficient path to get there.

One question that may come up is whether all this case management is really needed in every case. The answer is that the extent of case management needed depends on the clients and the case. There are certainly cases in which only basic case management is needed for compliance with court requirements, working through a narrow scope of open issues, managing limited action items, and memorializing agreements. Even in those cases that sail along with only light case management needs, the clients benefit from the mediator being able to efficiently shepherd them through from start to finish to quickly wrap up their case. In other cases, the clients do not anticipate needing much, if any, case management, but the need for more hands-on case management becomes clear later in the case. And then there are cases in which it is clear from the outset that the clients or the attorneys need strong case management to wrangle complex issues, personalities, or conflictual elements of the case to stay on track toward resolution. Having a neutral at the helm who can track both parties' details can be particularly helpful in such cases. In those cases, the mediator can follow any number of the steps outlined in this book to address and fill that need for case management to help the parties reach a mediated settlement and conclude their court case as efficiently and as thoroughly as possible, even under more difficult circumstances.

C. Inefficiencies in Litigated Cases

It is no secret that litigated cases rely on overburdened courts and an adversarial structure to slowly resolve the disputes of each case and plod toward finalization. Mediation offers an opportunity for more efficient and effective case management with the neutral professional guiding the parties and counsel from the outset of the case through entry of final judgment. To understand the limitations on efficiency in litigated cases and the benefits of neutral case management outside of court, let's take a closer look at nonmediated cases.

In litigated cases, separate attorneys often work as opponents within an adversarial process to manage the important substantive and procedural details to move the case forward. How well the attorneys work together impacts not only the tone of the case and how the clients experience the divorce process, but also the pace of progress toward final resolution. Counsel who are unable to prioritize efficiency or working well with other professionals may spend unnecessary time and professional fees on matters that could have been coordinated for a more streamlined process. For example, both counsel may file their own petitions to start the divorce in a case without good reason for a "first to file" approach and without considering the administrative inefficiencies and professional fees needed to consolidate the cases or dismiss one of the actions. Other examples include not participating in informal discovery, refusing to produce documents well within the scope of discovery, propounding antagonist discovery requests, refusing reasonable requests for extensions of time, or ignoring requests to discuss settlement issues, all of which result in delays without progress toward either of the clients' immediate or longer-term goals.

There are many examples of uncooperative counsel creating more work and slowing down or halting progress in the case. While not all family law attorneys are overly litigious, we have all encountered attorneys whose singular goal seems to be creating a combative environment without regard to the financial or emotional toll this takes on the family being dragged through the process. Unfortunately, many clients are unaware that hostile adversaries create more billable work for the attorneys without meeting the goals of the clients to reach an amicable and fair resolution and move on with their lives. In my experience, most respected family law attorneys know such behavior creates unnecessary hostility for the family and all the other family law professionals involved. On the other hand, when attorneys work well together, both clients benefit from their attorneys' ability to efficiently resolve discovery issues and work toward final settlement. This can be challenging when one attorney is reasonable and collaborative and the other attorney is a hostile adversary, which is why so many cases still end up in court despite the limitations on progress in litigated cases.

The courts in most counties offer a certain level of case management to parties and counsel and can act as a referee, which is helpful and even necessary in some cases, but has drawbacks in other cases. This is in part because the court typically is unable to closely manage the parties and their communication outside of court or manage the ancillary professionals involved in each case.

Without exception, the family law judges in the counties in which I have worked as a private mediator, court settlement conference mediator, and in my prior life as a litigator had an impressive grasp of the factual details of each case and the legal issues brought before them. With budget cuts to courts around the country resulting in substantial caseloads for family law judges, it is likely that the primary reason courts can keep so many cases moving through all the stages of each case in addition to presiding over short cause motions and lengthier trials is due to the court's reliance on exceptional jurists. Nevertheless, courtrooms with heavier caseloads result in less availability for hands-on management in any individual case. What this means from the perspective of the divorcing couple is that despite the expertise of judges, the court manages the parties and attorneys only during their infrequent appearances in court. Except for urgent ex parte requests, the court is generally not able to have more frequent case management check-ins on each of the discovery and settlement issues as they arise, whereas in mediated cases, when an issue arises, email responses and meetings can typically take place much sooner than would be possible in court. This is one of the gaps between the unpredictable needs of each case and what the court generally has capacity to provide.

It often happens that the progress in litigated cases is dependent on scheduling case status or motion hearings in which the court and the attorneys work on a limited number of issues on the court's full calendar. With the professional fees involved in preparing for and attending such hearings, often without substantial communication or progress in between hearings, this can lead to an excruciatingly slow pace, high professional fees, and dissatisfaction by the individuals involved in the case. Many family law litigators have had the frustrating experience of not getting the focused attention of the other party's counsel to coordinate discovery or begin settlement discussions until forced into a court hearing for a status conference or motion. Many such hearings could be avoided with more proactive (and responsive) case management. But, since separate attorneys tend to work in parallel as opponents under the court's management, there is often no cohesive plan for moving the case forward. This means there is generally less efficiency and productivity in court-dependent cases than in mediated cases in which everyone works as a team on an agreed timeline.

There are of course less contentious litigated cases involving productive working relationships between the attorneys and cases with lower conflict between the parties. In such cases, the attorneys are often able to work effectively outside of the limitations of the court's calendar and case management purview to resolve discovery issues, temporary stipulations, and other informal agreements as they work collaboratively toward settlement. But even settlement-oriented attorneys can find themselves in cases without movement on discovery or settlement progress and feel torn between escalating the case into litigation and hoping the other attorney or party will be motivated to start making progress without court intervention. This is where parallel lawyering and the adversarial nature of the court process itself becomes problematic for those wanting to collaborate to find a mutually agreeable and efficient resolution of the case.

Whether the case is higher or lower conflict, whether counsel is collaborating or not, or whether the court is providing discovery or case management oversight, common challenges remain. There is a higher likelihood that details might be missed, assumptions may be made in one party's favor, and the case can languish in litigated cases, given the conflicting interests and focus of the separate attorneys and the lack of a central management hub that goes beyond what the court can provide.

In mediated cases, the skillful case managing mediator can combine their family law and mediation expertise with the organizational and neutral mindset that is critical to efficiently guiding the clients and professionals through the maze of the divorce process in each of its stages. Because the mediator works for both parties and is on the same team as each party's separate attorney, the mediator and each separate attorney have a mutual client. As the neutral, the mediator works to balance the needs, goals, and interests of both sides (i.e., each client and their separate professionals) to create an agreed-upon structure and timeline for everyone and manage the details from a neutral perspective. As a result, missed details, misassumptions, and delays are less likely with a neutral professional guiding the case and all its participants through to completion. The neutral mediator helps the parties, the attorneys, and the court by serving as the nexus of information, details, and case management within the framework of the court case—but outside of the limitations of the court—to guide the case more efficiently through to final judgment.

It bears mentioning and keeping in mind throughout this book that not all cases can be managed, even by an experienced case managing mediator with years of successful mediations. Although higher-conflict cases can often benefit from having a case managing mediator, many such cases ultimately end up needing a decision maker and not a facilitator, and it can be challenging to properly vet these cases in the mediation intake process. In such cases, there might be emotional or psychological complexities with or between the clients that even the most case-managed mediation cannot overcome. Even though these cases will likely remain in the back of the mediator's mind for many years, I try not to think of these as failures of the mediator or of the mediation process, but as the result of an incredibly challenging family system that requires more containment and support than even a case-managing mediator can offer.

As mediators, we should also keep in mind that while the intricacies of the divorce process are well understood by the professionals, most clients facing the foreign world of a family law case may be overwhelmed, confused, and frustrated. Most clients appreciate being patiently guided through a difficult time and a confusing process and recognize how difficult their case could have been without the guidance of a neutral navigator. Experienced family law professionals typically recognize the mediator's heavy lifting on the case management and the resulting benefits to the professionals and their clients. Appreciative clients, counsel, and other professionals involved in the case who see the benefits of the case managing mediator's work frequently show their appreciation by referring other clients and professionals to the mediator. A win for them and a win for the mediator.

4

The Making of a Case Managing Mediator

The effective mediator does not need to declare themselves the case manager or impose a rigid case management structure. Instead, the mediator can educate clients and counsel about the case management that is typically helpful and what that might look like in their case.

In all cases, the mediator should develop a plan with the parties and professionals involved so everyone knows what to expect next. At the start of the case, the mediator can discuss what the mediator will be doing throughout the case at a high level, such as: "I will be working with you to start your court case and prepare your financial disclosures. We will then work together to create your overall settlement structure, getting into the details and brainstorming options together before we get to the stage of preparing your formal settlement agreement and submitting everything to the court at the end."

If there are attorneys involved at the forefront of the case, the mediator might say to counsel at the outset:

> I envision having a series of case management meetings with counsel to work on identifying the issues to be resolved, discuss any informal discovery issues, agree on a neutral forensic accountant and the scope of their work. We can also discuss discrete issues with the forensic accountant and put together a plan and timeline to make sure the parties have what they need to consider settlement options and proposals. We can decide together when we're ready to schedule mediations versus case management meetings. Does this plan work for both of you or is there something else we should consider?

In other cases, it may make more sense to just allow the case management to develop and occur organically. If the mediator believes a case management meeting might be useful during the case, the mediator can suggest something like the following: "We can exchange information by email and schedule a brief check-in meeting together to make sure everyone has the information needed before our next full mediation if that would be useful. Otherwise, we will just plan to meet as scheduled on May 1 for our next mediation." Offering the option of a case management meeting could work better in certain cases, such as: "We are scheduled for mediation in one month and we can schedule separate meetings [with each client and their counsel or with both counsel depending on what the mediator believes would be most productive] beforehand if that would be helpful to make sure we have all the information needed for a productive mediation and to get everyone ready for the joint mediation." Or: "It sounds like the attorneys are working on proposals for temporary support together and you can let me know if it would be helpful for us to schedule a meeting to discuss options together." While it is not always a case management meeting that is needed to manage the various steps in the case, having a plan and clearly identifying the plan and options to the parties and professionals is the job of the neutral case managing mediator.

If the mediator is comfortable in their case management role and is relying on their family law knowledge and understanding of the parties' and attorneys' goals, the mediator's confidence and neutrality will be telegraphed in all communication with the parties and the other professionals, building the trust that is so crucial to a successful mediation.

A. The Mediator as Team Leader

Being able to work collaboratively with the team of clients and professionals is an essential skill and responsibility of the mediator. Like any good team leader, the family law mediator needs to be a clear communicator; set and manage expectations; use empathy, integrity, patience, and emotional intelligence to build trust; build cohesiveness within the team; lead by example as a productive and respectful problem solver; and generally create order amid chaos. These goals can be accomplished by clearly identifying and organizing the parties' and professionals' shared procedural and substantive goals, mapping out timelines for discovery and settlement discussions, and keeping all the team members on track in a productive and supportive manner.

Instead of imposing rules or requiring action items as a judge or arbitrator would do, the mediator recommends action items and gets buy-in from the team members to ensure productivity and keep the case moving forward toward resolution. The mediator considers what work is needed to move the case forward and either suggests deadlines or seeks input from those who will be doing the follow-up work needed. For example: "I think Alex might need more than one week to finish the long-term budget that's been started with the financial advisor. Does two weeks sound more realistic? And would that also work for Ariel since we have discussed how important this step is for reaching complete agreements?" Or another example might be: "It sounds like having the two home appraisals needs to happen before either of you can consider the options we have discussed today. I know Judy is away for two weeks and you both want to keep the momentum going. Would you both be comfortable with John scheduling the appraisal inspections now or do you prefer to wait to get all of that started once Judy is back?"

It can be helpful for the mediator to refer to the group (clients and professionals) as a team, to acknowledge and motivate more great teamwork whenever possible. And the mediator can frequently use the collective "we" even when it's really "you" or "the two of you," such as: "I know we have been trying to reach an agreement on this one issue, but I'm wondering if we might shift to this other issue for a few minutes and circle back to this."

The mediator can also remind the parties of the supportive team they have put in place to help them navigate this process with language such as: "It's great to have such a collaborative team to be able to problem-solve together." Or, if the mediator needs to encourage more collaboration among the professionals, the mediator might say: "I want to encourage both counsel to bring down the adversarial tone and to approach this case more collaboratively, since that is what both parties have requested of us as the professionals in their case. I have worked with both of you in other difficult mediation cases and I know we can all work well as a team for the benefit of both parties."

It should be clear from these examples that the mediator is not chastising or berating anyone or otherwise using negative or judgmental communication even when someone on the team drops the ball. Instead of asking: "Why didn't you do what we all agreed you would do by now? You're holding everything up!" (which would do nothing other than pit that client or attorney against the mediator in a defensive manner, which is counterproductive to the mediation), the mediator can more productively ask: "Can you let us know what you have been able to do so far and how we can help get this timeline back on track?" And if there is hostility between the parties, the attorneys, or toward the mediator, the mediator might remind parties or counsel: "We are all working together to help our clients and there are going to be times when each of us is frustrated, but we need to be able to communicate respectfully in order to work together. Can we agree to make respectful communication a priority so we can make progress?"

Helping the parties and professionals work together as a team rather than against each other or even in parallel results in a more streamlined process in which issues are more efficiently and productively addressed and resolved. Creating a supportive, productive, and collaborative working environment allows a final resolution to be reached with less strife for the clients whose lives are at the heart of these cases and who are looking to the professionals to guide them through the case with the least amount of pain, time, and expense. If the mediator treats everyone like a member of a cohesive team, most team members can't help but start acting like they're part of a team as well. Others are not so cooperative regardless of the coaching of a supportive mediator; in those situations, the mediator can speak separately with the attorney to try to understand the source of the hostility, identify what appears to not be working, and guide the attorney toward more productive communication.

When separate attorneys continue to actively thwart a productive mediation process even after coaching from the mediator to support the mediation process, the mediator can decide whether to let their client know what seems to be getting in the way. And in either event, the mediator may decide not to work on future mediation cases with such attorneys and can remove those attorneys from their own referral list, given that such attorneys appear incapable of seeing how or why their aggressive tone or stances are getting in the way of meeting their own client's interests. In other words, there are just some people who will not be good team players no matter how much everyone else around them tries to get them onboard as a productive team member. Ultimately, if a client is aware their own attorney's aggressiveness is impacting the mediation, the client will likely need to decide whether to terminate the mediation or change attorneys.

As the team leader, the mediator is working in the trenches with the clients and the professionals to resolve issues and move the case forward. At the same time, the mediator also needs to be the voice of reason, remaining above the fray as the objective, neutral third party, offering practical guidance and helping both sides (clients and attorneys) to see all the issues and concerns in order to problem solve in a productive manner.

Many issues that arise can be resolved by the mediator clarifying any suspected confusion while remaining professional and neutral, acknowledging where both sides are coming from. Whether such issues arise in mediation, case management meetings, or email discussions, the mediator must be open to and curious about where both sides are coming from and not form immediate judgments about what a party or counsel may be saying or why. The mediator may be able to help clarify the issue via email while acknowledging both side's positions. In other situations, the mediator may suggest a brief check-in meeting to talk through the issues that arise and each sides' perspectives and figure out a solution on the issue together. Either way, the objective is to streamline the discussions, promptly resolve the concerns, and not let arguments or positions take over and turn the case into a battle by email.

Recognizing the signs of a discussion on the brink of disaster and identifying solutions to get the discussion and case back on track helps pave the path toward a successful overall outcome for the parties. For example, an unraveling email dispute between counsel about temporary support calculations could be managed by the mediator in various ways, such as: "It seems like it might be helpful to schedule a meeting with counsel to identify the differences in your calculations and figure out what we can get agreements on for temporary support. I am available at the following times. . . ." Or maybe the mediator sees the problem and can offer a logic-based solution that might appeal to both counsel, such as:

> I ran my own support calculations to try to figure out the discrepancy between your two calculations and I think it might be the result of the following two assumptions. . . . I understand why you each included what you did in your own calculations based on X and Y reasons. Given the circumstances and stage of this case, it might make more sense to treat these issues in manner A rather than manner B or C due to the following reasons. . . . I have attached the mediator's compromise calculations to this email and you can let me know if this would work for both of you and your clients or if a meeting would be helpful to discuss this together.

If an email discussion starts to unravel into unproductive combat or other ill-advised attempts at mediating via email, the mediator can step in to organize the discussion or schedule a meeting. Bringing calm and professional organization to anger and chaos is one of the many ways the mediator manages the case and all the individuals involved as the team leader. In certain situations, this can be accomplished with the mediator's email lead-in, such as: "If we can take a problem-solving approach, I see the following options. . . ." Or if more coaching is needed: "I recognize this is a sensitive issue, but I am hoping we can keep our discussions focused, respectful, and productive. To that end, I would like to suggest the following. . . ." Of course, this kind of reminder may be easier to use when both clients or counsel have "forgotten their manners" in their written or verbal communication, but it is still supportive and fairly nonjudgmental and can be used even if just one client or counsel has slipped into accusations or other unproductive communication.

As a rule, I prefer to minimize "mediating via email," which occurs when there are back and forth emails to resolve settlement issues. At its best, this can help efficiently close out discrete issues or identify issues for discussions in a meeting. However, mediating via email can also create avoidable complexity, bringing misunderstandings and frustration that can carry through into meetings. Many clients choose this approach based on their assumption that emails will be faster and less expensive than a meeting, but this is often not the case. Such email discussions can incur substantially more professional time for the mediator to organize and interpret what is being said and to write detailed responses to questions that can be more thoroughly addressed in a meeting with less professional time required.

Nevertheless, the occasional mediation by email will present itself. If an email discussion is productive and not overly time-consuming to interpret and track, the mediator does not need to discourage it but might respond with a hint of caution, such as: "If you prefer to work back and forth by email on these issues for now, we can continue as long as it works for both of you and is productive." If the clients are particularly cost sensitive, the mediator might add: "though it would likely be more efficient if we scheduled a meeting to work through these open issues all at once since these issues need discussion, which is more time consuming by email than in a live discussion."

If there are signs of productivity unraveling in the email discussions, including accusations or inflammatory or otherwise negative communication, the mediator can step in with more direction about the process, such as: "In my experience, mediating by email particularly on issues like this is not the most productive or cost-effective way to reach agreements. I suggest that we find a time to meet in the next week or two to address the time-sensitive issues that are causing concern for both of you. I can be available at the following times. . . ." Or the mediator might make an even more direct observation with a particularly challenging dynamic, such as: "It is clear that mediating by email is not working, and we need to schedule our next mediation to work through these issues together. My office will circulate dates. Thank you." If the clients decline the mediator's suggestion to meet, the mediator may need to consider whether the clients are the right fit for mediation, because continuing to work with clients who do not trust their mediator or the mediation process will continue to create issues that are not in the parties' (or the mediator's) best interests. It can be helpful to remember that if the clients could reach agreements without the help of a mediator, they would have already done so at their own kitchen table or the coffee shop.

If one party seeks to control the process and decide what happens next or how the meetings are structured, neither party is getting the benefit of the neutral mediator's expertise in guiding the two parties through this difficult time in their lives. This can be a challenging situation to manage. Ultimately, the mediator needs to be confident in their own role and to be comfortable inviting the clients to change course when the goals of one or both parties are not aligned with the mediator's role as the neutral guide for both parties through this process. In other words, the mediator works to create order out of disorder and provides a supportive process that is not rigid but adjusts for the needs of each case, provided the mediator is not restricted by one or both parties from doing the work they have been engaged to do.

The mediator also needs to be able to work well with many different personality types. This means making an effort to hear and understand each of the individuals, to hear the concerns raised by their attorneys (or recognize the concerns underlying a position), and to problem solve with the team. This may include mediator suggestions to counsel, such as: "Jennifer may not be comfortable recommending this to her client because it leaves her client exposed and Adam feels like this is the only option to protect his client. What if we were to create just an interim agreement on this so Adam's client has protection for the next two to three months while Jennifer's client is protected from the open-ended exposure she is concerned about?" Or maybe a more open-ended starter is needed, such as: "Would it be possible to look at this from a different angle? How else might we tackle this?" I particularly like bringing the issue and responsibility for helping to solve the dilemma to the parties or counsel themselves, such as: "I don't want this issue to stop all the progress that has been made here. Do either of you have any suggestions on how we might resolve this so we can move forward?"

The mediator can elicit agreements from the parties and professionals to support the team in navigating the process together and always know what's happening next. For example: "Are we all in agreement that these three things need to happen before our next meeting? Is there anything else we need to add or does this sound like a good plan for now and we'll reconvene in three weeks?" Throughout this book, we will continue to explore ways in which the mediator can employ and hone these case management skills for the benefit of the parties, counsel, and the mediator.

B. Communications Expertise and Ongoing Education

Most successful mediators I know are strong communicators with natural curiosity, empathy, and patience. The foundation of a mediator's effectiveness in each case is their ability to:

- Communicate clearly in person and in written correspondence.
- Organize the substantive case details.
- Keep track of the procedural requirements.
- Memorialize proposed and agreed settlement terms in a neutral manner.
- Manage action items for everyone involved to ensure the case progresses toward completion.

- Do all the preceding while ensuring neither side is (or feels) disadvantaged and while preserving positive relations and communication with all individuals.

Managing the various personalities and needs of the clients and the professionals, keeping on top of the substantive and procedural issues of every case, and keeping everyone on track in a neutral and productive manner requires frequent and ongoing productive communication. If communications by the mediator are perceived as abrasive, impatient, or lacking empathy, problems will arise. To be an effective and empathic mediator, the mediator needs to genuinely enjoy communicating with and helping individuals from various backgrounds and cultures and without judgment as to the nature of the parties' relationship or the reasons for their separation.

The effective case managing mediator likely has a diverse background, which may be the result of their natural curiosity, and that certainly influences their skills as a mediator. For example, I started my college education in journalism and worked as a private investigator throughout college and law school. Each of those paths supported the curiosity, intuition, and communication skills on which I have relied in my mediation practice for more than 20 years. As another example, a long-time friend and family law mediation colleague is a musician and great-grandfather with a fascinating array of life experiences, and whose authenticity, fluidity, and empathy as a person has influenced his nearly four decades as a mediator. Other mediators with busy, successful practices tend to bring qualities of curiosity, empathy, and patience to their mediations as well as their life experiences; this may include being entrepreneurial trailblazers, artists, therapists, military leaders, philanthropic board members, international mediators, world travelers, or just professionals with specific interests and passions. As a result of these diverse backgrounds and life experiences, successful mediators are able to connect to individuals and hold space for different viewpoints and personalities to guide clients through a difficult process with compassion and empathy.

In addition to being a strong communicator, the family law mediator truly needs to have a vast amount of legal knowledge and expertise. This requires not only time and experience handling family law cases and other types of cases, but also requires the mediator to embrace being a lifelong learner. I don't think of our education as mediators as a stage of arrival, but rather as an ongoing approach to life; we have graduate degrees and professional licenses, but we also continue to educate ourselves in countless and varied ways as individuals, which elevates our mediation practices and ultimately benefits the individuals with whom we work.

These areas in which we continue to educate ourselves should include not only family law, tax law, and real estate law, but also various areas of psychology, including relationship research, neuropsychology and behavior, child development, LGBTQ+ perspectives, and substance abuse, just to name a few. Many of these topics are included in continuing education courses available through local bar associations, statewide organizations such as California's Association of Family Law Specialists (AFCLS), national organizations such as the Association of Family and Conciliation Courts (AFCC), or international organizations such as the International Academy of Family Lawyers (IAFL).

Mediating attorneys and non-attorneys should keep current with changes in state and local family law and recent caselaw. In addition to core family law updates, family law mediators also need to be informed about current events, politics, finance, and economics. This ancillary knowledge enables the mediator to connect to the parties and professionals and may even be directly relevant to any number of settlement issues, including recent or looming layoffs for a big corporation or industry impacting support issues, changes in tax law, highly anticipated initial public offerings, mergers, or even significant changes in the stock market due to political shifts.

Because full-time mediators are not litigating court cases, they are typically not spending time in court hearing the rulings by local judges. Family law mediators can keep up to date with their local family courts and judges by attending local continuing education courses and other local family law events, which are frequently attended by non-attorney family law professionals in the counties in which we practice. Local family law events help mediators keep a finger on the pulse of the local family law bar and bench to hear about and discuss trends in court rulings, what judges are seeing or are struggling with, and knowing what changes are on the horizon for the counties in which the mediator practices. And of course, it's never a bad idea for the mediator to socialize professionally with other members of their local family law bar to remain at the forefront of their minds when they are considering involving a mediator in their next case.

C. The Flexible and Curious Mindset of the Mediator

Curiosity, a flexible mindset, and intuitiveness are musts for mediators. Rigidity is anathema to any successful mediation practice since a rigid process or mindset does not allow the mediator to forge a new or creative path for their clients. That can only be accomplished with a mediator curious and maybe brave enough to make suggestions that are out of the ordinary or significantly different from what a court might order. A flexible mindset allows the curious mediator to explore what might be going on internally or between the parties that may be preventing a productive discussion. In addition, it may allow for the discovery of options not yet considered or that are hard to envision without a little exploratory work.

Curious mediators allow themselves to explore questions at every stage, whether procedurally, structurally, or substantively. Examples of internal questions the mediator might consider include: "I wonder if it might be better to meet separately before the joint session given what their attorneys have told me? I wonder why their prior mediation or collaborative process didn't work? I wonder why his response to that seemed guarded? I wonder if a different support structure would make more sense given their personalities? I wonder why this is such a big issue? What if we flipped this whole thing upside down and looked at it completely differently?"

Curiosity can lead to questions posed to the parties that may resonate with one or both parties in pivotal ways. One example might be: "Would you both be open to hearing an idea that's quite different from the way the court would approach this issue? If not, we can move on, but I wanted to put this out there if you are both open to considering a different option." If both clients answer in the affirmative, then the mediator can explore the option with them. If one client says no and one says yes, the mediator might explore both parties' reasoning so they can each hear the other's concerns and have a conversation about their preferred approach. The mediator leads such discussions without judgment and can even express that if appropriate, as in: "There is no judgment on this since there is no single right or wrong way of resolving this. I just want to make sure we're considering options that might work better than what we have been struggling with."

Curiosity might lead to options the parties didn't think were feasible, such as: "Have you considered what it would look like if you didn't sell the house right now? I'm wondering if you might be open to discussing some other ideas on this." Or: "There may be other options here, such as using the separate property retirement account to create the liquidity you both need and rebalancing the other assets in a different way. There are special tax rules in divorce, and we can talk about options if this is a path you both want to explore."

Curiosity can also lead to observations that open up the discussion and get at the heart of what's behind one person's hesitation on an issue or other observations about the big picture, such as any of the following:

- "I get the sense that something didn't sit well with you just now, Henry. Would you be willing to say more about that so Pat can understand what's going on for you?"
- "There seems to be a lot of tension in the room today. Can you tell me a little about what's happened since our last meeting since it seems like we're not gaining traction on any of the topics today?"
- "Can we talk about what's going on between the two of you that seems different than in our prior meetings since it seems to be impacting the settlement discussion today?"
- "I have the sense that neither of you want to be here today and that's ok. Do we want to talk about rescheduling or figure out what's getting in the way?"

These types of discussions can often lead to better understanding and maybe even compassion between the parties that can help soften rigid positions, minimize anxieties getting in the way of productive settlement discussion, or even break through roadblocks to settlement. The possible paths these conversations can lead to are endless.

D. Allowing Intuition to Guide the Mediator

How does the mediator know:

- When to intervene and when to step back?
- When to push back on settlement positions?
- When to make suggestions or recommendations?
- When to ask personal questions and when to refrain?
- When to allow the clients to process information or consider proposals and when to push the conversation forward?
- When to meet separately or jointly during or before a joint discussion?
- When or how each client will be best able to hear an alternative perspective or proposal?

We all have some level of intuition that gives us hunches or signals—sometimes faint and other times blaring. These signals might be conveyed through nonverbal communication the mediator observes, such as tone of voice, body language, or facial expressions. Other times, there is no apparent reason for the feeling the mediator picks up, but is more of a "sixth sense." Having taken on the role of guiding both parties through the challenges of their case in the context of often intense emotionality, mediators need to pay attention to these signals and allow their intuition into the mediation. The mediator's intuition can guide the mediator throughout the case, but only if the mediator is paying attention. The more we pay attention to our own intuition, the stronger and more apparent those signals can become, because we are honing one of the communication skills needed to be a good mediator.

Intuition is often described as knowing something without knowing why you know it. According to experts in human development, intuition "is a form of unconscious intelligence that is as needed as conscious intelligence."[1] Intuition and emotional intelligence go hand in hand and are as important to the mediator's abilities as retaining legal and factual details, and being able to logically analyze problems, organize details, and communicate with different personality types.

While some mediators are trained as both lawyers and therapists, having such dual training or expertise is not required to become a great mediator. However, an attorney–mediator does need to be psychologically minded so they are attuned to what is or is not being said by the clients or counsel, and are able to gauge and respond to the emotional shifts in meetings and emails.

Starting out with new mediation clients, it can be helpful for the mediator to describe their own communication style up front and to check in periodically on the pace of the meeting or their saturation levels. In my mediations, if I suddenly think I may be speaking too quickly or I notice one party's eyes glaze over or I see a perplexed look, I pause and take a breath because I know I have subconsciously picked up on something. I then ask how the pace feels (too fast or slow, or just right?). I ask if there are any questions about what I've just said. And I might check in about how both parties are feeling before I resume with any new information in mind.

Details about both parties' education and employment backgrounds are often helpful for the mediator in communicating with both parties. If the mediator is working with two fast-paced CEO-type individuals who are used to absorbing and processing large amounts of new information, everyone will likely enjoy a quick pace. If the clients both tend to speak slowly or take time to consider and process information before moving to a different question, they will likely benefit from a slower pace. This may reflect their own personalities, their education levels, or just the type of work they do, regardless of baseline I.Q.

Even if the mediator has figured out the right pace for the clients, the mediator still needs to pay attention to uncomfortable shifts, signs of

---

1. Psychologist Gerd Gigerenzer, Max Planck Institute for Human Development in Berlin, cited in *8 Truths About Intuition*; author Matthew Hutson; *Psychology Today* Magazine, January 2020.

confusion, emotions bubbling up, or other clues that something needs an adjustment. If not addressed, one or both parties may not be able to hear what is being said if they are struggling with something internally or are afraid to speak up to identify their concerns. This can lead to a party not truly being engaged in the mediation and leaving the mediation feeling they had a negative experience, even if they can't pinpoint the reason. As an example, the mediator may sense that one or both parties have hit their limit emotionally in a meeting. This might be the mediator's own observation that the parties look wiped out well before the end of the meeting. Or perhaps the discussion devolves from a productive brainstorming and negotiation session to an unexpectedly exasperated "I just don't know" or multiple monosyllabic responses. These may be clues that one or both parties (and maybe even the mediator) have reached their saturation point and it will not be fruitful to press on in the discussion at this moment. Such clues call for a quick check-in, such as: "How is everyone feeling right now—do we want to move into the retirement account discussion now or are you feeling we've hit our limit for today?" If one party is ready to press on but the other is not, the mediator may want to encourage reconvening when everyone is in the frame of mind to be able to productively mediate. This kind of balancing is commonly needed by the mediator, who needs to be attuned to signals from either party that something is or is not working in the moment and to adjust accordingly.

Intuition may lead the mediator to recognize the need to give one or both parties time to breathe, cry, or process what's been said or what is happening between the parties. Intuition may also lead the mediator to suspect that a different meeting structure would work better in one case than in another case. If one party seems to have disengaged or there are frequent emotional flares, depending on the overall circumstances, the mediator might suggest separate meetings, such as: "I am thinking it might be helpful to have separate meetings with each of you before we continue this joint discussion—how does that sound?"

In addition to being a useful guide in mediation sessions, intuition can also guide the mediator in email correspondence as well as with respect to the timing of an email response. Often, an immediate response can help reduce brewing friction. Other times, the mediator may sense that a cooling off period would likely be beneficial for everyone before the mediator intervenes.

Toward the end of a particularly difficult mediation session, instead of just plowing ahead and scheduling the next mediation, the mediator might identify what they are observing, such as: "It seems like today was a really difficult discussion and maybe we need to put a pause on this for a few weeks; what do you think?" Or: "It seems like there wasn't enough time for you to both consider all the issues between our last mediation and today. Do we want to talk about scheduling our next mediation now or do you both prefer to take a little breathing space and email me when you're ready to schedule our next meeting?" Making these observations and suggestions helps the parties to know that you see what they're experiencing and are there to help them navigate the process and adjust to their unique needs, which is why this is such an important principle in basic mediation training.

Keep in mind that signals and clues might arise at any time, including in the initial mediation session when everyone is still getting comfortable with each other and the process, or it could occur several meetings in or even toward the end of the case. Either way, the mediator needs to be attuned to what is happening for both parties and anticipate and adapt to emotional shifts that can affect the settlement discussions.

Not only is the flexible and curious mindset of the mediator important in the brainstorming process of settlement negotiations, but it is also critical to maintain flexibility as to how the case will conclude.

E. Case Managing with Patience

As an organized family law professional, it may be helpful to keep in mind that our clients—regardless of their education levels or the skills required for their own professions—often misplace documents or portal passwords. Our clients forget information, including when or why tentative agreements were reached. Or they can simply feel overwhelmed by the volume or density of information in their cases or the pressure they feel to make important decisions.

As case managing mediators, our role is to guide both parties through the process with understanding and patience. Family law, and family law mediation in particular, are not typically our clients' fields of expertise, and by hiring us, they have requested our expert guidance. Mediation clients have other jobs and responsibilities they are often excellent at performing. Excelling in other aspects of their lives does not typically translate to clients being organized and efficient managers of the substantive and procedural issues in their own family law cases. Even if our clients are highly organized, these skills do not enable our clients to view their case from an objective perspective given their role as a party to the marriage and the pending divorce.

If the mediator has the sense that either client is feeling lost, overwhelmed, or just not sure what is happening next, the mediator should pay attention and address the concerns. Options for adjusting the structure or process in such circumstances might include any of the following:

- Figure out how to simplify or streamline the steps for the clients. Break things down and find out what works for these clients.
- Ask if there is a different format that might be more useful for them. For example, some clients have a harder time following narrative summaries and prefer spreadsheets (or vice versa). And some clients find they cannot think in joint meetings and need to schedule separate meetings to be productive in the mediation.
- Suggest a call or meeting to discuss issues that arise in email.
- Discuss the best way of sharing/obtaining information or communicating and patiently walk the clients through what is needed in a way they can understand.

It is important that both parties know the mediator is hearing their concerns or relying on their mediator's intuition to sense that there might be a problem or that an adjustment could help the process. Knowing the mediator is paying attention to their concerns and is there to guide them when they get a little lost along the way, even when the clients don't know how to communicate that they are feeling lost, is an important part of establishing the parties' trust in the mediator's ability to guide them through the process in the best way possible.

F. Managing Project Managers

Effectively working with clients who bristle at being managed can be part of the mediator's role in keeping the case on track. Project managing clients with higher emotional intelligence often accept the guidance of an experienced case manager. There can even be a sense of relief for these clients knowing they are in good hands and recognizing that each step of the process is being identified, managed, and followed through to completion. Other project managing clients may not be able to recognize the expertise of anyone as being more useful than their own sense of what steps should happen, in what order, and in what structure, regardless of their inexperience in family law; this often leads to frustration by everyone involved.

While the mediator's intake and vetting process can be structured to eliminate most of the hostile or combative potential mediation clients—clients who do not believe they need guidance, or who would otherwise not be a good fit for mediation—these individuals still slip in. This may be the result of "interviewing well" by the potential clients or it could be changed circumstances outside the mediation process. Either way, the mediator needs to determine and maintain their own professional boundaries about what the mediator will and will not accept from mediation clients or other professionals involved in the case. When the mediator is comfortable with their own role and boundaries, there can be an honest assessment of the personality fit for mediation at the outset of the case. This helps the mediator to clearly articulate their role in the case and what the clients can expect if one or both parties tries to control the process. Maintaining these professional boundaries is often a career-long aspiration for mediators who are passionate about helping individuals in these cases.

Similarly, the mediator often needs to balance client requests to structure the mediation process with the mediator's own experience and intuition. For example, a request for separate sessions in lieu of joint sessions may be a request the mediator carefully considers. The mediator may ask for brief, separate discussions regarding the structure before making a decision with the parties. Or the parties may prefer to mediate via email despite no forward progress in that forum, or their joint or separate mediation sessions may be unproductive, and the mediator may suspect a different structure could be more fruitful for their settlement discussions. In such situations, the mediator can guide the case into a more productive format, whatever that may be for the individuals in the case.

On the other hand, if the mediator requests a meeting with the attorneys or to schedule a check-in meeting with the clients and one of the parties refuses such a request, the mediator can identify the purpose of the requested meeting and let the clients know why it is important to the overall mediation process and progress toward a final resolution. If a client still refuses the mediator's request, the client is restricting the mediator's ability to mediate, which generally leads to no progress and benefits neither client in their goal of reaching a mediated settlement.

If the clients insist on their own structure and want to direct the process to their own detriment, the mediator is not required to be a participant. Follow-up emails in such situations could signal that the mediator is leaning toward terminating the mediation, such as:

> The purpose of engaging a mediator is to guide you through the process to reach complete agreements and conclude your court case. While you are the decision makers on every substantive issue, the mediator's role is to structure the process to best support you in reaching agreements based on the mediator's expertise. If we are going to work together to meet your shared goals of reaching a mediated settlement, it is important that I can manage the process as I have been engaged to do. I look forward to hearing from both of you to confirm you are aligned with the purpose of my role as mediator.

> If this is not the role either of you envision from your mediator, we can discuss other options, including a different mediator or ending mediation completely. Thank you.

If mediation clients repeatedly reject the mediator's guidance on the mediation process itself, the mediator should feel comfortable in accepting that it is not a good fit between the clients and the mediator to work together. This is not a personal or professional failure by the mediator, but is an experience the mediator can rely on for signs to pay attention to in vetting future potential mediation clients.

Not every set of mediation clients is going to be a good fit for each mediator. In the intake and vetting process, the mediator should consider both potential clients' personalities, how the parties communicate together, how each party communicates with the mediator, and the extent to which each party is open to accepting guidance from the family law professionals they have engaged to do just that. If the mediator is not looking forward to working with the clients, the mediator should consider referring the case to a different professional who may be a better personality fit or whose process is structured differently than a case managing mediator's process might be structured.

G. Avenues to Becoming a Family Law Mediator

Ask three family law mediators how they handle and manage their cases and you may receive three different answers. This is often the result of how the mediator came to mediation in the first place, in addition to their specific mediation training, their background in family law, and their primary mediation style.

Although backgrounds, mediation styles, and approaches differ among experienced and well-respected mediators, we do not see many mediators with a central ongoing role guiding each case from the court case initiation through entry of final judgment. Instead, family law mediators tend to take the more traditional settlement-conference-approach to mediation. In this approach, the separate attorneys are responsible for all premediation workup, financial disclosures, discovery, case management, drafting agreements, and finalizing the case and related steps, while the mediator is solely responsible for the day of settlement negotiations. The mediator typically holds separate "caucus"-style meetings in which the mediator shuttles between the parties and their counsel and the parties have no direct contact. This structure reflects the traditional format of mediation in civil cases and is often the structure expected from the professionals in family law cases. But this structure limits the ability of the mediator to manage and positively impact the case from the outset, to set the case up for productive settlement discussions, and to see the case through final judgment as the neutral case manager.

There is no singular "right" style for a family law mediator. The style of family law mediation that works for my office may not work as well for another mediator. Because each case and set of clients has different needs, it is worth the time for the parties and counsel to find the right mediator for each case based on the specific needs and personalities involved in the case as well as the background, style, and case management approach of the proposed mediator.

So how do family law professionals become mediators? Some litigators find themselves collaboratively resolving cases well before the pressure of trial forces a settlement. These attorneys may find themselves being asked to work with both parties in one case and then another, organically developing a neutral mediation practice. This is how I found myself becoming a mediator more than 20 years ago and well before I received formal mediation training. I found that I had the desire and at least some innate ability to hear both parties and help bridge their differences, and these existing qualities needed to be strengthened and refined with training and experience. When I encounter family law attorneys in whom I recognize the same innate facilitative problem-solving or empathic peacemaking qualities, I encourage the advancement of their mediation skills and offer to discuss the development of their own mediation practice as much as possible.

While there is a need for other types of mediators as well, my perspective is that there are not enough of the peacemaking, empathic, problem-solving mediators practicing family law mediation, but I hope this will change for the benefit of the family law community and the families we all serve. These mediators are often the helper personalities, whose compassion and desire to help drives them into mediation. These mediators are the mediators I most frequently see organically taking on case management responsibilities, though they may not realize the extent of the case management they could be providing to benefit their clients and the professionals involved in their cases.

Another common avenue to becoming a mediator is long-time battle-weary litigators seeking a less-combative approach to resolving cases after decades in the trenches of trial work as a second career or an easing into semi-retirement. These attorneys tend to bring an authoritative and directive law-based approach to their mediations and are often well respected for their litigation expertise and knowledge. These mediators tend to excel in evaluative/directive-style mediations, in which the mediator directs settlement by evaluating the legal merits of the case based on the law and the facts, typically working separately in caucus-style, full-day mediations. A reputation as a skilled and ethical litigator lends gravitas to the litigator turned mediator. Such mediators are often sought out by family law attorneys who recognize the need for an expert litigator in the role of an evaluative and reality-checking mediator to settle certain cases like a private settlement conference judge.

There is often little to no case management provided by this category of "litigation mediator," since such cases tend to proceed similarly to a litigated case. Formal discovery is conducted by separate counsel and settlement briefs are provided to the mediator in advance of the mediation. Similar to traditional civil mediations, at the end of the long day of mediation, the attorneys prepare a term sheet for parties and counsel to sign before leaving. Afterward, the attorneys start the work of drafting the formal settlement agreement, with the attorney for one party taking the first pass at the initial draft and the other attorney proposing edits. There are typically back-and-forth edits and proposals until there is a final agreement on the language of the formal agreement. If disputes arise in the drafting and editing stage of the formal agreement in these cases, the attorneys will either meet to try to work out the details or they may propose a follow-up mediation with parties and counsel to resolve such issues. If the parties signed an enforceable term sheet or Memorandum of Understanding (MOU) and the deal falls apart in the drafting of the comprehensive formal settlement agreement, either side may file a motion for enforcement of the MOU. Once a final draft is approved by both parties and counsel, one of the separate attorneys takes responsibility for preparing and filing the judgment submission with the court and may provide updates to the other counsel and party about such steps. In such cases, the separate attorneys will also assign responsibility for managing any actions triggered by the signing of the settlement agreement or entry of judgment, such as drafting and filing Qualified Domestic Relations Orders (QDROs) for retirement transfers and real property transfer deeds. Although this is the traditional mediation style employed in civil mediations as well as family law, there are benefits to including neutral case management in these cases, including:

- The mediator can suggest case management or discovery meetings to set the case up for more productive settlement discussions, including pre-mediation meetings and case management meetings between mediation sessions to keep things on track.
- The separate attorneys can request additional case management from the mediator at the outset of the case so the mediator can manage action items, discovery issues, and get to know the interests of the parties and counsel in the context of each case.

- After agreements are reached in mediation, the mediator or attorneys can request the mediator's involvement in the formal drafting stage, including drafting the initial comprehensive agreement from a neutral perspective, managing drafting disputes as they arise (rather than waiting until the deal has completely fallen apart to seek neutral case management), and overseeing the signing of final agreements, QDRO and real estate transfer processes, and conclusion of the court case alongside the separate attorneys.

Retired judges seeking to wind down their legal careers may also call on their decades of experience to help families resolve cases as private mediators in addition to private judging in jurisdictions that permit the appointment of a private judge in place of the public court. Some retired judges bring impressive conflict resolution skills and emotional intelligence to their private mediation practice in addition to their wealth of knowledge, and can deftly move along the continuum of primary mediation styles, from facilitative to evaluative, dipping into transformative, and back again. Other retired judges—like many long-time litigators—may rely more heavily on a directive judicial settlement-conference-style in private mediation and the respect from the family law bar as an authoritative and knowledgeable voice. In private mediation, it is more common for retired judge mediators to employ shuttle diplomacy with separate caucusing rather than joint mediation sessions. Like long-time litigators turned mediators, in cases with a retired judge as mediator, the representing attorneys are typically involved in the forefront of the case to prepare the case for mediation or trial while the mediator focuses exclusively on settlement negotiations, similar to a settlement conference judge, and are not typically involved in the case management suggested throughout this book. Nevertheless, I encourage separate representing attorneys to request the involvement of the retired judge mediators from the outset of the case for all the reasons already discussed as to why clients and counsel benefit from having a neutral case manager throughout their case. Retired judicial officers might consider the benefits of neutral case management for the cases in which they are engaged and can suggest or raise as an option this level of involvement, even when the attorneys do not make the request directly.

In addition to these more common paths to mediation, most law schools now incorporate alternative dispute resolution (ADR) in their curriculum. This means there is a new generation of attorneys who may graduate with a solid foundation in mediation (if not family mediation specifically) that was not as available to those of us in previous generations at that stage in our legal development. This may eventually lead more lawyers into ADR fields like family law mediation, though there are currently very few law schools offering family law mediation education or training. This is the foundational experience of my mediation partner, Shelley Kennedy. A mediator of 15 years, she graduated from law school with more mediation training and dispute resolution coursework than most mediators accrue during their mediation careers. There are more mediators with similar backgrounds now—mediators who have dedicated their training and career to mediation—honing their dispute resolution skills rather than their adversarial skills. Despite not being trial attorneys before becoming mediators, these family law mediators are able to provide effective case management and family law expertise throughout their cases in addition to their unique perspective from outside the traditional litigation framework.

Of course, not all family law mediators are lawyers. The family law mediation field, from its earliest inception in the 1930s with California courts offering conciliation services, has always been multidisciplinary. Therapists, social workers, child development experts, educators, accountants, and family court personnel worked together with even greater cross-disciplinary collaboration with the founding of the AFCC in the 1960s and the founding of the Academy of Family Mediators (AFM) in the 1980s.[2]

As attorney–mediators, I believe we should support non-lawyers' involvement as custody mediators, financial mediators, and as general family mediators helping families and courts in countless ways. As family law professionals, there will be opportunities for collaboration among mediators from different disciplines and we can continue to learn from each other to improve our mediation skills and practices in countless ways. We should continue to build each other up, to promote other deserving professionals, and to minimize any territorial feelings that may get in the way of unexpected collaborations that benefit our clients, our fields, our communities, and our own individual practices.

H. Training and Practice Development for Family Law Mediators

Despite the prevalence of mediation in family law cases, most law schools in the United States do not offer family law mediation courses or clinics. Of the almost 200 accredited law schools in the United States, many offer basic family law classes, civil mediation, and other dispute resolution courses or clinics in these areas, but only a small handful currently offer courses or clinics

2. Marquette Law Review, Volume 95, Issue 3 Spring 2012 Article 8, *Lawyer Colonization of Family Mediation: Consequences and Implications.* Debra Berman and James Alfini; AFM was a precursor to the current Academy of Professional Family Law Mediators (APFM), which was formed in 2012 after AFM was merged into other mediation organizations.

in family law mediation. Even in California, which is known for its strong encouragement of mediation and was one of the first states to adopt formal family mediation programs in the courts in the 1970s,[3] only four of the 21 ABA-accredited law schools offer family law mediation courses or clinics.[4] So, how do attorneys and non-attorneys actually become family law mediators?

While there are currently no uniform requirements in the United States for using the designation of "mediator," the California State Bar is currently working to establish certification requirements for mediators and arbitrators, and other states continue their own efforts on this front. It is not yet clear how this might impact the many non-attorney mediators who work in the family law field. However, most successful family law attorney–mediators I know have a minimum of two 40-hour mediation trainings, including skills-based community and general mediation civil trainings, and at least one 40-hour family law mediation training, in addition to family law experience, which could include many years as a mediator or a combination of family law litigation and mediation experience.

Regardless of the extent of family law experience, without the training and reinforcement of basic mediation skills and tools in these intensive 40-hour trainings, the mediator is limited to their own intuitive sense of how to manage each unique set of clients and professionals. In my own mediation development, I mediated without formal training as it organically took shape in my law office so long ago. In my first 40-hour general mediation training, when asked why I was there, I said something along the lines that: "I want to understand why what I'm doing without training works and how I might be able to improve what I'm already doing by learning more mediation tools."

I highly recommend participating in multiple 40-hour mediation courses taught by different professionals to get the benefit of varied and unique perspectives. As is often the case with teaching a course or hosting a training, I have also benefited greatly by being a trainer in multiple mediation trainings; such experiences force the trainer to consider why certain strategies may be more or less helpful in a given situation, further honing the mediator–trainer's own skills.

Although I spent years litigating civil litigation and family law cases before fully transitioning to mediation, one of the most important steps I took to further develop my family law knowledge base was to study for and take the family law specialist exam through the State Bar of California. Being

---

3. *Id.*

4. UCLA School of Law, USC Gould School of Law, Loyola Law School, and Pepperdine Caruso School of Law.

a family law specialist certified by the State Bar of California requires a certain number of trainings and practical courtroom skills experience in addition to passing a "mini-bar exam." While I believe I could still be a strong family law mediator without this experience and designation, it is just another increase to the stable of knowledge and skill that a mediator can bring to their own practice. Other family law mediators may choose to obtain their LLM in mediation or taxation. Others work to obtain a CFA (certified financial analyst) or CDFA (certified divorce financial analyst) designation. Mental health professionals may earn more advanced degrees (MFT, MA, PhD, etc.) in addition to mediation skills training and family law-specific trainings to further increase their knowledge and skill for the benefit of their clients.

Although mediation training courses provide a critical foundation, the second most important aspect of practice development for the mediator is experience. The more the mediator mediates, the better mediator they become. There are mediation opportunities in most counties for small claims or community mediation programs that are not related to family law but provide the opportunity to mediate in multiple settings and with different personalities. Opportunities to obtain family law mediation experience also exist, with many counties offering free or low-cost mediation services to qualifying low-income individuals; such programs rely on family law mediators offering their services, often in exchange for the experience of mediating various family law issues.

While some counties offer free or low-cost mediation services to all litigants regardless of their income levels, I have mixed feelings about the impact on mediators and the field of private mediation when there are no income thresholds for providing free services. Such programs encourage the reliance on experienced family law mediators to offer their services for free while the separate attorneys (and court personnel) are compensated at their normal rates. In addition, even when progress is made in the limited time available (typically between two and eight hours in a single day can be offered by such programs), the participants are precluded from engaging the mediator privately to continue what may have been the first bit of progress in the case. My feeling is that such income-blind court-based structures undermine the professional work and practices of private mediators, since there is little reason for an inexperienced litigant to pay an experienced private mediator for their services when they can access the very same mediators in the free program offered by the courts, even when the parties have substantial wealth. Nevertheless, when a family law mediator is first starting out, there are limited opportunities to gain experience, and income-blind programs offer at least that much as a benefit to new mediators. I believe that court-based mediation programs that include income thresholds offer a more stable path of experience for newer mediators that is less destructive to the private mediation field as a whole and should be supported by family law mediators whenever possible.

I. Developing a Family Law Mediation Practice

Starting any new business endeavor involves a leap faith and some kind of financial security, at least for a certain period of time while things get going. I won't get into the basics of opening an office, marketing, branding, networking, or creating a website and content, as those are a given for any new business. What I can offer is the following specific guidance to developing a family law mediation practice:

1. Complete one or more 40-hour mediation training courses before reaching out to other mediators to get their advice on getting started. This signals that you are serious about becoming a mediator, having spent the time and money for the course fee (in addition to the lost time at work!) toward this goal.
2. If you are not a family law attorney, find and complete multiple family law courses for therapists or financial professionals. The AFCC and the Association of Professional Family Mediators (APFM) are two options for finding such courses.
3. Contact two to three mediators whose practices or styles you respect or admire and let them know where you are on this path and why; find out if they have any suggestions for upcoming trainings, mediation programs, or networking events. Offer to take them for lunch, coffee, or drinks to talk about your plan and any advice they may have for you based on their own path and your specific goals.
4. Unless you are in a practice with other mediators, you may want to join or establish a professional consulting group to discuss issues that come up in your mediations, particularly when you are the only neutral or even the only family law professional in the case. Consulting groups can be hard to create and harder to sustain given the challenge of balancing busy work schedules and the need for everyone—even experienced mediators—to generate income to pay their bills and fund their lives, so creating mutual benefit here is key.

5. Another option is to engage a mentoring mediator or consulting mediator to brainstorm issues, options, and strategies in your cases. The specifics of such fee-based arrangements can be worked out between the professionals and can be case specific or include a once a week or twice a month standing consultation time, for example, to discuss various hypothetical situations and not just one specific case. Veteran mediators have a wealth of knowledge and practical experience to share and should be considered as a resource for any mediators. Newer mediators and solo practitioners can also benefit, since they often do not have the benefit of multiple mediators working in an office who can offer this kind of ongoing strategy and support to help with individual cases as well as practice building.
6. If you are a family law attorney hoping to transition fully to family law mediation, but you are still accepting new representing clients, I recommend setting a boundary that ensures the only new cases you accept are the ones you want in your mediation practice. Continuing to take litigation cases while you are hoping to be a full-time mediator is incongruous both in practice and with respect to the mediation skills you are not honing while you are continuing to battle for one party in court. The skillset of a litigator is not compatible with the skills and qualities of a mediator, which include relying on and embracing intuition, compassion, and balancing the needs and interests of both parties in every action and every word spoken or written. The family law mediator needs to continually practice these skills and hone the natural qualities that already exist in their own personalities to ensure they bring the best version of their peacemaking, bridge-building, and problem-solving selves into each case regardless of their backgrounds. But every time the litigator argues a point or pushes an argument in court or traditional settlement conferences, the litigator further hones their adversarial skills and taps deeper into the combative aspects of their personalities, pushing them further from their goal of becoming a mediator.
7. Decide what case management tools you wish to incorporate into your practice. While there are family law-specific and ADR-specific tools for managing cases, there are currently no applications specific to family law mediation case management. Case management tools can include time and billing management as well as calendaring, applications for managing compliance with state and local requirements in each case, and managing the various other procedural and

substantive issues in each case. It can be helpful to ask other family law mediators what they are using and take the free demos to see what works best.

8. Work on improving your skills in Excel, Word, Google Docs, Google Sheets, and any other applications frequently used by family law mediators and attorneys in your area. Even if you have assistants, these basic skills are helpful for efficiently working through issues in mediation with the team. There are other programs that can be useful for family law mediators or their offices, such as Family Law Software, Xspouse, Clio/Lawyaw, Essential Forms, and so on, to explore and decide what will maximize efficiency for the mediator and clients and what is an unnecessary cost.
9. Join the APFM and attend their virtual meetings and networking sessions. This is an incredible organization of other professionals throughout the world who are passionate about doing this work with varying perspectives and practices, including attorney–mediators, financial mediators, mental health mediators, and other non-attorney mediators. I have had wonderful discussions through APFM with mediators from Canada, Australia, and throughout the United States that further inspire my own work and passion. I highly recommend becoming an active member.
10. Join the local chapter of AFCC and attend their in-person events to join other like-minded interdisciplinary professionals working to help families through the difficulty of divorce.
11. Embrace being a mediator. Learn about it. Read about it. Write about it. Speak about it. Enjoy it!

5

The Mediator as the Central Hub

While the key benefits of mediation certainly include the skilled facilitation of settlement discussions in mediation sessions, the importance of the neutral mediator is not limited to just settlement negotiations. The mediator has the opportunity to serve as the central hub of information and guidance for the parties and the professionals. The mediator can manage the substantive issues and steps needed to advance the case toward completion while navigating the unpredictable needs of each case and balancing the needs of everyone involved from a neutral perspective. In this way, the mediator can steer the ship (i.e., the case, the clients, and all the professionals) through all the stages of the case through and often beyond entry of final judgment.

A. Case Initiation Documentation in Every Case

The mediator should always have the eventual drafting of the formal settlement agreement (or Memorandum of Understanding or term sheet) in the back of their mind, even at the outset of the case. To start the settlement agreement or term sheet later and minimize the number of blanks to be filled in and the number of draft agreements to be circulated, the mediator should always start out by ensuring all court case initiation documents are in the mediator's possession.

Regardless of whether the court case was initiated prior to mediation or with the mediator's assistance, or whether the mediator is an attorney or non-attorney, as the neutral case manager the mediator should ensure the parties and counsel have electronic copies of all case initiation documents at the outset of the court case or the outset of the mediation. Ideally, the mediator will be the host or manager of a password-protected document vault or portal to which only the parties and professionals in the case have access.

The documents the mediator and all other participants should have at the outset of the case include the following filed documents:

- Petition
- Summons
- Proof of Service of Summons
- Response
- Proof of Service of Response
- Any other filed state or local forms related to the case initiation, including judicial notices and scheduling of status conferences

Once filed and served (or once obtained), the mediator can share the complete set of case initiation documents with clients and counsel as the central information hub. The mediator will be able to use these court case initiation documents to confirm the start date for any minimum waiting period and the trigger dates for completing financial disclosures, and to discuss preferences regarding timing for marital status termination. This helps the mediator begin getting alignment on these issues with the parties and counsel and working toward common goals.

If any of these initial documents are not available at the outset, the mediator should work with the parties, their counsel, and sometimes with the parties' prior mediator to obtain and share these documents with the team. Failing to obtain the filed case initiation documents could result in delays in the court's approval of the final judgment at the end of the case if any filings are incomplete. The only way to know there will not be an issue later in the finalization of the case is to ensure there are no problems at the outset of the mediator's engagement. And, since memories fade and practitioners retire, best practice is to secure and share these with the team up front so there are no loose ends or delays when it comes time to wrap up the case. This can be of particular concern when court processing deadlines for end-of-year judgments are at issue. Scrambling to obtain missing documents (or to prepare declarations when prior professionals are no longer available to verify service) at the last minute is not best practice for any of the professionals involved, particularly when all of those steps could have been completed at the start of the case. My preference is to not make everyone crazy at the 11th hour before filing a request for final judgment. Instead, I prefer to nudge the professionals (or their staff) and procedural steps along at the outset to ensure the file is complete and the judgment at the end is not vulnerable to a procedural misstep that could have been caught at the start. I typically send an initial request to the attorneys with the list of documents needed (from the court's register of actions or just based on general knowledge of what should be available) and then have our legal assistants follow up about once a week until we've managed to obtain what we need.

In fast-moving cases in which separate attorneys have started the court case prior to mediation and agreements are reached quickly in mediation and are being memorialized into a settlement agreement, I tend to be the one badgering counsel for anything still needed that could slow down the court's judgment processing. This might include an email, such as:

> I am just following up on this thread since we sent the draft agreements out today and will begin working on the judgment documents but we are still waiting for Richard to provide the filed Proof of Service of Summons and Sam to provide her client's filed Declaration of Preliminary Disclosure so our judgment request doesn't get held up. Please let us know if you need our office to do anything to help with these two items. Thank you both.

This advice to identify at the outset what will be needed at the final stages of the case applies to other case initiation details as well. This includes confirming domestic partner registration details, consolidating or dismissing duplicate proceedings, confirming that financial disclosure declarations have been filed with the court, or checking that attorneys or self-represented parties' addresses are accurately reflected in the court record, and determining who is attorney of record instead of consulting counsel. Addressing the court's procedural requirements up front avoids delays in judgment processing at the end when there may be more urgency to obtain the clients' final judgment. And while some counsel or parties may be reluctant to spend time on these details, as family law practitioners, we know what each court requires, and we know what happens if the court does not receive what it needs. There is no reason not to ensure each of the procedural steps required to finalize the divorce are complied with early in the case to ensure a smooth procedural path to the finish line.

When the mediator is brought into a pending case rather than at the outset, the mediator should also request documents beyond just the case initiation documents. This includes premarital or postmarital agreements; financial disclosures; and any other motions, current orders, or other filings. The mediator can start by checking the court's register of actions (which is usually available online) to determine what has already been filed before discussing what information the mediator may or may not need to do their best work. In counties without online registers of actions, the mediator can request from the parties or counsel a list of documents filed with the court and make a decision as to what would be useful for the mediator and ask the appropriate party or counsel to provide it. Keep in mind that motions and orders can be critical for the mediator to review in certain cases, while in other cases it is less important from the mediator's perspective depending on the number and nature of such motions prior to the mediator's involvement. It is worth considering what is needed before requesting and reviewing every filing, depending on the needs of the case when it comes to mediation.

B. Variations on Mediator Filings and Communication with the Court

One of the key differences between settlement-conference-style mediators and case managing mediators is that when the latter is an attorney, the case managing attorney–mediator typically files pleadings and interacts with the court on behalf of both parties, while the former does not.

Case managing attorney-mediators may draft and file the case initiation pleadings, financial disclosure declarations or statements, stipulations and orders, settlement agreements, and judgment documents at the end of the case. Settlement-conference-style attorney–mediators typically leave the formal drafting and filing to the separate attorneys, which leads to all the challenges previously raised about the adversarial system and lack of a neutral voice in the initial drafting of formal agreements.

Non-attorneys can also serve as case managing mediators with some adjustments on the mechanics of the court filings (including the option of teaming up with an attorney–mediator). Even if non-attorney mediators cannot file pleadings on behalf of their clients, non-attorney mediators can maintain the same role of drafting detailed term sheets or initial draft agreements for later attorney input and filings to the extent possible based on state law, tracking the filings even if submitted by someone else, and providing updates to the mediation team of clients and other professionals from a neutral perspective.

There are some courts that still maintain purely adversarial filing structures and do not permit filings from a neutral mediator (whether attorney or non-attorney) because the mediator is neither a party to the case nor one of the parties' separate attorneys of record. In those courts, filings by the mediator typically need to be made on behalf of only one party, which is at odds with the neutral role of the mediator working equally for both parties. When the neutral mediator is forced to prepare a document for both clients to sign that has only one party in the caption and that is then filed with the court, the other party can feel sidelined or otherwise feel they are not being jointly served by the neutral mediator. Even if there is no conscious recognition of this by the omitted party, there can be a subconscious feeling that can permeate other aspects of the mediation and jeopardize the outcome.

In certain counties, the mediator can only file on behalf of both parties as their neutral attorney–mediator unless there are attorneys of record (i.e., attorneys who have appeared in the matter on behalf of the individual parties). In such circumstances, the agreements and other filings prepared by the neutral mediator typically need to be filed by one party's attorneys. But requiring a neutral document prepared by the mediator to be filed by one party's attorney can alter both clients' sense of the mediator's neutrality. It can also shift the responsibility of managing the filing and any requests by the court or follow-up needed from the neutral professional to one party's separate attorney. This workaround by the mediator may satisfy the existing adversarial court structure, but it negatively impacts the mediation efficiency and how the parties and attorneys view the mediator's neutrality. As attorney–mediators, we can continue to encourage our local courts to support private mediation and create pathways for efficiency for the parties, the court, and mediators by ensuring neutral attorney–mediators have online case access and the ability to file joint documents on behalf of both parties, whether or not there are representing attorneys, in each case.

Some courts are more progressive when it comes to the involvement of private attorney–mediators. And while the local rules for each county vary, mediators can often file a stipulation or declaration informing the court that a neutral attorney–mediator is involved in the case. This can pave the way for the mediator to file pleadings and otherwise communicate directly with the court on behalf of the parties, including receiving and managing court notices and requests.

One of the counties in which we practice in the San Francisco Bay Area[1] has a helpful local form titled "Stipulation for Appointment or Removal of Mediator (Family Law)" (see Figure 5.1). With this local form, the parties can easily let the court know they have engaged a mediator, provide the mediator's contact information, and grant the mediator access to the court file. This same form is used if either party elects to no longer participate in mediation or when the mediator is no longer mediating the case for any reason, including upon conclusion of the court case.

Since many other counties in which we practice have not yet adopted similar local forms, we have created our own Stipulation for Appointment of Private Mediator (we have added in the word "Private" to our own pleading to distinguish this from court-based mediators) based on the simple and clear

1. San Mateo County local form FL-18.

Figure 5.1 Stipulation for Appointment or Removal of Mediator (San Mateo local form FL-18)

ATTORNEY OR PARTY WITHOUT ATTORNEY (Name, State Bar Number, Address) TELEPHONE NO: FAX NO.(Optional): E-MAIL ADDRESS (Optional): ATTORNEY FOR (Name):	FOR COURT USE ONLY
San Mateo Superior Court, Hall of Justice 400 County Center Redwood City, CA 94063	
PLAINTIFF/PETITIONER: **DEFENDANT/RESPONDENT:**	
STIPULATION FOR APPOINTMENT OR REMOVAL OF MEDIATOR (FAMILY LAW)	**CASE NUMBER:**

We, the undersigned, have elected to participate in collaborative law, or mediation, to resolve our case and grant remote access of the case file to the mediator.

☐ We hereby stipulate to ______________________, as mediator.

Mediator Name ____________________
Address ____________________
____
____
Phone Number ____________________
Bar Number ____________________

I, the undersigned, have elected to no longer participate in collaborative law, or mediation, to resolve our case.

☐ I hereby remove ______________________ as mediator.

I, the undersigned, am no longer providing services as Mediator in this matter.

☐ I hereby remove myself as mediator.

Dated:

______________________________ ______________________________
TYPE OR PRINT NAME SIGNATURE

Dated:

______________________________ ______________________________
TYPE OR PRINT NAME SIGNATURE

Form adopted for Mandatory Use
FL-18 – Adopted 3/5/21

STIPULATION FOR APPOINTMENT OR REMOVAL OF MEDIATOR

www.sanmateo.courts.ca.gov

language of the San Mateo local form FL-18. As soon as we are engaged in a pending case, we file our Stipulation for Appointment of Private Mediator with the parties' and any representing counsel's signatures. If the court case has not been initiated yet, we include this stipulation for the parties' signatures with the other case initiation pleadings and file these concurrently. At the end of our engagement, we file this document with the "removal" language included.

In prior years, we used to submit a self-prepared Declaration Regarding Mediator to notify the court of the attorney–mediator's involvement. However, including the same information in a short stipulation signed by the parties rather than the mediator's own declaration makes it clearer to the court that the parties have requested the mediator's involvement. This encourages the court to provide the mediator access to the court file, to allow the mediator to file pleadings on behalf of both parties, and to communicate with the mediator regarding filings.

In the San Francisco Unified Family Court, there are currently two local forms the mediator can file that are less streamlined than the San Mateo stipulation referenced earlier, but essentially operate in the same way: (1) SFUFC-11.14-A Declaration Authorizing Court Communication and (2) SFUFC-11.9-B Declaration Re Acceptance of Service at "In Care of Address," if the mediator's address will be used for the parties. In San Francisco cases, our office still uses both declarations to comply with their procedures and ensure our office receives all court communications during our engagement. Following the conclusion of our work in the matter in these cases (i.e., typically upon entry of final judgment), our office files Notices of Change of Address for both parties (which the parties sign when they sign their judgment documents with our office) so that any postjudgment communication from the court is directed to each party directly. While this is not as streamlined as the Stipulation for Appointment of Private Mediator, it's what this court currently requires and so we comply.

My hope is that court clerks and judges may be relieved to see informational pleadings regarding the attorney–mediators' involvement to know the case will likely require only minimal attention from the court when the final judgment request is made at the end of the case. If more attorney–mediators are taking these steps in their own cases, we can hope the courts will continue to make room for attorney–mediators' involvement to shepherd these cases through the system. One way the courts can help is by creating their own local forms to identify private mediators, provide authorization for the court to communicate with the mediator, provide online case access, and permit the mediator to file joint pleadings on behalf of both parties (regardless of whether there are also representing attorneys), and to allow for the mediator's withdrawal by either party or mediator, given that private mediation is a voluntary process. A single local (or statewide) form such as this supports one of the many shared goals of the courts and private mediators: to minimize acrimony and streamline the process and costs for the parties, their families, the attorneys, and the courts.

C. Managing Status Conferences with the Court

Status conferences (aka case progress conferences or hearings) are typically short hearings for the court to check in on the status and progress of the case and determine what needs to happen to move the case toward settlement conference or trial. Status conferences often require far more time for both parties or their counsel to travel to and from the court and sit in the courtroom waiting for their case to be called just to have a 5- to 20-minute discussion about the case status. While some courts have retained options for virtual appearances following the required virtual attendances during the COVID pandemic, many courts have returned to prepandemic rules requiring in-person attendance for such hearings. This means the time and cost for attending such a hearing can outweigh the benefits of the short hearing, particularly in cases with a case managing mediator who is moving the case forward outside of court. Filing a short stipulation requesting a continuance of these hearings is generally the preferred option in actively mediated cases and is typically offered as a local form in each county.

The mediator can track, calendar, and follow up with clients or counsel on such hearings and deadlines for submitting requests for continuances. And the mediator can prepare and file stipulations requesting to continue such hearings on behalf of both parties. When representing attorneys are involved, the separate attorneys often take the lead in filing requests to continue status conferences. In either case, as the case manager, the mediator should always keep track of these hearings, keep an eye on the court calendar for any changes, and coordinate with the parties and any counsel to reach agreements regarding continuances. This could be a simple check-in with representing attorneys, such as: "The deadline to continue the August 1 status conference is next Friday. Please let me know if you are working together to request a continuance based on the progress being made in mediation or if you would like to schedule a brief phone call to discuss options including the duration of the continuance to request." The attorneys may either respond that they will handle the continuance filing or they may request input from the mediator.

In cases in which the attorneys' request for continuance of a status conference was previously denied (meaning the court is not seeing sufficient progress without judicial involvement), the mediator might suggest specific language to include in a follow-up request to provide the court assurance that the case is progressing since the last status conference. One example could be to identify the mediator who has since been engaged if the mediator might be known to the court and to give a more substantive update, such as this example, which has worked in such cases: "The parties engaged private mediator Paula Lawhon on 7/5/2025 and have made substantial progress toward finalizing their settlement terms. The parties are working to memorialize their agreements in a formal Marital Settlement Agreement with their mediator and counsel." As always, the mediator's office should track any updates in the court's calendar, including any orders granting or denying the continuance, and can follow up with the attorneys on next steps.

In cases without attorneys, the mediator might give a little more information and guidance, such as:

> The court has scheduled a case progress conference in your case for September 1 to ensure your case is progressing. Based on the open issues we are still working through, I recommend that we request a 120-day extension to give us enough time to work through the remaining open issues, prepare your formal agreements, and submit your judgment packet to the court before the hearing. The deadline to continue the case progress conference is August 16. Please let us know if you are both comfortable with the suggested 120-day continuance and we will prepare the stipulation for your signatures and file this with the court prior to the August 16 deadline.

For non-attorney mediators, these same principles of tracking, managing, and following up on status conferences and any other court requirements also apply, with the understanding that the parties may be submitting filings directly to the court unless the non-attorney mediator has teamed up with an attorney–mediator for this purpose. As an example, the non-attorney mediator might send this follow-up to clients: "Your status conference with the court is scheduled for September 15 and since our next mediation is scheduled for September 8, you may want to continue this hearing for 90–120 days. Please let me know if you are both comfortable with this plan and you can fill in the timing for the request in the attached Stipulation before you sign and submit to the court before the September 5 deadline or you can have your consulting attorneys prepare and submit this for you."

The mediator should ideally be involved in every aspect of the case as the neutral guide through each stage. If the mediator is not responsible for a particular component of the case, they should still know what is happening and what the procedural status of the case is. Imagine working with clients to help them resolve all of their issues, drafting a formal agreement (or detailed term sheet), and then discovering the court dismissed the pending case for failure to bring the case to trial or failure to appear at multiple hearings on motions or other requests for order. Regardless of background or licensing of the mediator, everything is interrelated in family law mediations, and the mediation process should never set the clients back in their progress toward completion. This means the mediator—whether attorney or non-attorney—should be aware of any aspects of the broader case, even if not directly related to the specific topics being discussed in mediation.

Every aspect of a case has the potential to impact every other aspect. This is why a custody mediator needs to know what is happening in the financial mediation and vice versa. And why a co-parent counselor needs to know if there are upcoming hearings or motions on financial issues that may impact the parents' ability to productively work together on their custody schedule. Or why an accountant–mediator needs to know if a motion has been filed or if the case has been pending in the courts long enough that the court could dismiss the case without good cause shown as to why the timeline for finalizing the case should be extended. Or why a legal or financial mediator needs to know the progress or challenges occurring in the custody mediation.

As the case manager, the mediator should be the central nexus of information and management on all issues. Once the mediator understands how each facet of the case is impacted by all other components in the case—legal, financial, interpersonal, and parenting—the mediator can feel more comfortable ensuring they are up to date in each area with the understanding that updates aren't always offered but need to be sought out by the mediator. It is not uncommon for a co-parent counselor to ask about the status of the financial negotiations or the legal case only to be met with a response by clients or counsel that this is outside of the scope of their work with the parties. The mediator's response can be that each element and stage of the case impacts the parties and their discussions on other matters, and it is helpful for each neutral professional to know what else is happening. This information can come from the clients, or the professionals can check in together to ensure they are all up to date. With that in mind, starting each meeting with an update on any court deadlines, an update on co-parenting or other meetings, and otherwise asking how the clients have been doing and communicating outside of mediation can be a helpful check-in for the mediator. This allows the mediator to keep a finger on the pulse of what else is happening that may affect the overall mediation or the immediate discussions that day.

D. Referring To and Managing Other Professionals

A good mediator is always open to hearing the needs of the parties and empathizing with their situation. The mediator who truly listens can be a trusted source of information to help the family in whatever their needs may be. This often means the mediator is providing referrals to clients for ancillary professionals related to any number of issues in the case. Referrals might be made to parenting specialists, forensic accountants and other financial advisors, health insurance brokers, mortgage specialists, home appraisers, estate attorneys, tax attorneys, or even separate family law attorneys.

Experienced mediators typically have a list of their own trusted professionals to recommend, but should always keep in mind the personality fit based on the needs of the individuals. For example, if the mediator sees that a client needs more gentle and patient hand-holding, we do not refer them to the fast-talking tax advisor, but will instead make sure the client gets to the advisors we know to provide a more holistic and patient approach. Or, if we have a hard-charging client, we pair them with an advisor on their same communication wavelength for an optimal match.

In addition to referring clients to professionals, there are often situations in which the mediator recognizes that a partner in the overall mediation process could be beneficial for specific clients. For example, in a case in which parenting issues are front and center and additional support may be needed to get the clients started, the mediator might refer the clients to a custody mediator before beginning discussions in the financial or legal realm. Other times, including situations involving traumatic events in the marriage or mental health issues for the parents or their children, the situation may call for an initial joint meeting with the financial/legal mediator and the custody mediator to discuss and agree on the roles and overall process at the outset as well as to determine the viability of mediation for the specific situation. Before recommending parenting or other neutral mental health professionals, the level of conflict and support needed should be considered as well as whether the professional has experience or is open to co-mediating if the financial/legal mediator believes that structure would be useful in the particular case.

In other situations, hearing and understanding the needs of the clients does not lead to a referral and instead leads the mediator into a deeper exploration of new ideas or options regarding the relationship or finances for the couple to consider. A great mediator keeps an open mind and maintains a fluid approach within a structured process, guiding the discussion where it needs to go depending on the needs of the parties.

In addition to making referrals, the mediator should be involved in engaging other neutral professionals to ensure the neutral professional is provided with a neutral scope of the planned engagement. This includes jointly engaged financial or legal experts as well as neutral parenting professionals. The mediator can make suggestions for professionals who may be a good fit for the parties, can make introductions including the proposed scope of work, can schedule an introductory meeting, and can coordinate the engagement process to keep things moving efficiently forward. If a stipulation regarding allocation of fees and/or for appointment of a jointly retained expert is needed, the mediator can draft this from a neutral perspective for the parties' and attorneys' review, input, and signatures.

Once other neutral professionals are involved in the mediation, the mediator maintains their role as case manager, ensuring the other professional has everything they need and is kept abreast of all updates in the case. Some cases call for a co-mediation structure in which two mediators are engaged jointly and have equal responsibility for managing the parties and the process. There are also multidisciplinary situations in which multiple neutrals (for example, an attorney–mediator, co-parenting mediator, and a joint forensic accountant) work together with one clear case managing mediator. An accountant mediator and legal mediator might serve as neutral co-mediators with the two mediators attending each mediation session and collaborating on all correspondence and case management throughout the case. Alternatively, an attorney–mediator may engage a neutral forensic accountant for a limited scope as an ancillary neutral consultant without a plan to co-mediate or co-manage the case.

The mediator should keep in mind that a plan for another neutral to start out at either end of the continuum between co-mediator and neutral consultant may change over time and any such professionals might end up assisting in an adjusted role in the mediation if the need arises. I have often had cases in which we bring a neutral consultant into a case for a limited purpose, but discover a greater benefit in having the two neutrals working more closely as co-mediators to help the parties reach complete agreements.

In any case in which the parties or counsel are considering engaging another neutral, the mediator should first identify and communicate the scope of the anticipated work to ensure everyone is aligned on expectations up front. In my own cases, if I anticipate co-mediating with a forensic accountant or parenting professional, at the outset of any such collaboration, we discuss the following:

- Our respective roles.
- How we plan to structure meetings—whether there will be any separate meetings with the parties or counsel or whether all meetings will include both professionals.

- Whether each professional will send separate emails without input from the other. While the answer to this question is usually yes, it still warrants the neutrals discussing the overall plan up front to avoid misunderstandings, overstepping, or confusion of the respective roles between the neutrals and by the other mediation participants.

There are some mediators who have worked as their own solo ship captain for so long that even when a co-mediation structure has been agreed to, one or the other mediator neglects to include their co-mediator on correspondence or to let them know when milestones have been reached in the case. For example, in one co-mediation with a parenting professional and an attorney-mediator, the attorney-mediator neglected to inform the co-parent counselor that complete agreements were reached and that the settlement agreement was signed. This resulted in the parenting professional—who was supposed to be co-mediating—left feeling their role or input was not valued.

As a reminder to the parties and counsel of what has been discussed about the joint engagement and also as a reminder to those long-time solo mediators who might otherwise forget or not recognize the importance of the "co-" in "co-mediation," it can be helpful for the mediators to send a joint email at the beginning of the engagement to set everyone's expectations. With a custody co-mediator, the email might include something like this: "Because Marit and I will be working as co-mediators in this case, it is important for the integrity of this process that we are both included on all emails and in all meetings regardless of the topic unless everyone agrees otherwise." Or with a forensic accountant as co-mediator, the email might indicate something along the lines of the following: "We have all agreed that Rick and I will be working as co-mediators in this case. To ensure we are all as efficient as possible in working through the document requests and production and discussing settlement issues, please be sure we are both copied on all emails to minimize the need for us to reconcile and fill in any gaps outside of our mediation sessions."

In my practice, co-mediators are on equal footing in all respects regardless of the sphere of expertise of each mediator. For example, when I am co-mediating with a psychologist, all meetings and correspondence are conducted jointly based on the overlapping, interrelated parenting, legal, and financial issues. This is also part of the containment that the two professionals working together can provide and the unique benefits of having a mental health expert to identify any psychological issues impeding productive settlement discussions. Nevertheless, even when clients have signed an Agreement to Co-Mediate that outlines this structure, we still experience clients or counsel asking to meet with one or the other or emailing just one of us based on their assumptions that each professional handles their own separate sets of issues.

As a result, we typically work to ensure the co-mediation structure is clear at every stage possible and just add the other co-mediator to any email thread when they have been omitted. I might also send a gentle reminder, such as: "I have included Stacey on this email thread since our co-mediation structure relies on the collaboration of the two professionals on all of these issues and we have included below our availability for our next meeting." I also include both co-mediators' names at the end of all joint emails as a reminder of the joint structure and the fact that we collaborated on the email for the benefit of the clients and the process.

In cases that are not co-mediations but have other professionals actively involved, the mediator still needs to align everyone's expectations and identify everyone's role. For example, in a case with a neutral financial professional, some clients or counsel might assume the neutral financial professional will prepare the parties' financial disclosures, but that may not be the core reason for engaging the financial professional. And there may be good reasons to have the attorney–mediator or separate counsel prepare the financial disclosures so the financial professional can focus on more specific projects.

In other words, there are numerous assumptions about what each professional's role might be with respect to individual steps in the case, and the case managing mediator needs to identify those steps and work with the team to decide which professional will take on each step. This avoids duplicating time-consuming work, including but not limited to financial disclosures. I have had the experience of discussing with clients their preference to have my office prepare their financial disclosures only to find out both parties' separate attorneys were also working on the financial disclosures for each of their clients, resulting in unnecessary duplicated expense. When clients have separate counsel but have agreed to have my office complete their disclosures, we make sure their attorneys know; otherwise they are paying multiple professionals to do the same work, which is one of the things most clients want to avoid.

This is one of the reasons a clear follow-up email to clients and any counsel is helpful after a meeting, to identify all steps and clarify who is responsible for each task based on the meeting with the clients. When clients are not sure how to decide on something like this, the mediator can suggest a check-in call with the attorneys to discuss and agree on the preferred manner of handling that step and any others for the benefit of the parties and the process.

Although follow-up emails and mediation summaries are discussed in further detail in Chapter 9, it is helpful to note in this section on other professionals that follow-up emails to clients identifying action items and next meetings should also be shared with the other relevant professionals in the case. This typically includes separate family lawyers, but may also include the neutral or separate forensic accountants and estate planning counsel, depending on the nature of their roles in the case, and of course any co-mediators and other parenting professionals. Other more tangential professionals like real estate appraisers, business valuation experts, one party's own personal financial advisor, or other limited-scope professionals are not typically included in these follow-up emails. However, to manage everyone's expectations, the mediator should discuss with the team who should be on those email distribution lists, keeping in mind that sometimes those lists change throughout the mediation. The mediator should maintain a system for keeping this information updated throughout the case.

6

Impeccable and Reliable Financial Disclosures to Support Mediation

Complete and accurate financial disclosures are critical to a successful mediation and an enforceable settlement agreement. Since the mediator may be engaged at any stage in a case, the exchange of financial disclosures might take place prior to the engagement of the mediator or may not have taken place yet. This chapter will include options for both scenarios as well as other ways the mediator might organize the necessary details for the mediation and drafting the formal agreements as the case-managing mediator.

A. Mediator-Prepared Disclosures

At the outset of the mediation, if financial disclosures have not yet been exchanged, the mediator can focus the parties on information gathering to prepare the parties' separate disclosures, so this information is available in settlement discussions. If there are separate counsel involved, there will need to be coordination to ensure no duplication of time and efforts by the clients or professionals.

One of the benefits of having the mediator prepare the financial disclosures is that the mediator can ensure that sufficient details for the discussion and future formal agreements are included for each asset and liability, including account numbers, institutions, title holders, statement balances, loan details, and the supporting statements that reflect all those details. These are the details the mediator and clients will need in the settlement discussions and for the eventual drafting of the formal agreements. The format that works best for my practice is the following:

- Bank of America checking (account *1234) in both parties' names; balance as of 12/31/2025 statement: $25,689.
- Fidelity brokerage (account *5678) in both parties' names as trustees of the John and June Brown Family Trust; balance as of 12/31/2025 statement: $130,230.

- Morgan Stanley Trust (account *9112) in June's name as trustee of the June Brown Separate Trust; balance as of 12/31/2025 statement: $212,512.
- Roth IRA held with Morgan Stanley (account *8585) in John's name; balance as of 12/31/2025 statement: $18,500.
- Inherited IRA held with Fidelity (account *9131) in June's name; balance as of 12/31/2025 statement: $300,850.

It is important to remember that although many clients start in mediation assuming both spouses know the same details about their finances, that is often not the case. One spouse might manage the parties' accounts while the other has limited visibility for various reasons. There might be different account types that each party has managed within the relationship. Both parties and the mediator need basic information about how many accounts there are (rather than "checking accounts $50,000"), which accounts are jointly titled or separately titled, and in whose name the deeds and mortgage are held. Without this information, there is a lack of transparency, which can lead to a sense of information and power imbalance that can impact the viability of the mediation, including interfering with settlement discussions as well as the effective drafting and enforceability of formal agreements. Ensuring everyone has the same level of information and documentation supports the overall mediation. The sooner these details can be provided, the more transparency will exist to level the information playing field, allowing both clients to move more comfortably and efficiently through the mediation discussions.

Another benefit of mediator-prepared disclosures is that because the list of assets and liabilities is verified by the statements and documents provided, there will be no inconsistencies between the parties' lists of assets and liabilities. This ensures the mediator can rely on the disclosures in settlement discussions and in preparing settlement calculations and formal agreements because the work has already been done to ensure the disclosure details are complete and accurate with supporting statements. We have likely all started mediations with client-prepared or even attorney-prepared disclosures without account numbers, institutions, or types of accounts included and have needed to spend time reconciling each party's separate list of accounts without enough information to do so. This can be easily resolved in mediation when there are just a few accounts; however, the more accounts there are, the greater the need for specificity coming into the mediation at the outset. Working through these details together with the parties in mediation has the added benefit of maintaining transparency between the parties.

Mediator-prepared disclosures can streamline the professional time needed for gathering information, preparing the draft disclosures, and compiling the exhibits. Since a single set of exhibit files will support both parties' separate schedules of assets and liabilities as a reflection of their entire estates, whether or not an asset is titled in one party's sole name, this can save substantial time.

While some separate attorneys may be reluctant to have the mediator prepare the separate schedule of assets and liabilities because it is not prepared solely for their individual client, mediator-drafted disclosures can be reviewed and edited with separate counsel prior to each party signing their own separate disclosures and providing these to the other party and counsel. The exchange of financial disclosures can take place through the separate attorneys or through the mediator, depending on everyone's preference, but the mediator should still ensure that any required declarations related to the financial disclosures—whether prepared by the separate attorneys or the mediator—are signed and filed with the court to comply with local or statutory requirements.

Although each party will sign their own set of disclosures prepared by the mediator, each party's separate schedule of assets and liabilities can be identical to the other party's schedule since all factual details should be supported by the exhibits; any opinions or positions before resolving an issue can be noted as just that. In the example of real property with a question as to whether one party has a separate interest or claim, we might include: "1234 A Street, Townie, California, 98765, held in both parties' names as trustees of the Adams Family Trust; encumbered by a Bank of Marin mortgage (loan no. *4321) in both parties' names. Current FMV *TBD; Susan indicates $100,000 down payment was made with her premarriage funds *TBD details." Or, if the parties agree to the amount of separate property to be considered at this stage, that last section could just identify it as "Includes Susan's $100,000 separate property down payment." Or, if the clients have already agreed on a fair market value for the home in which they have used an adjusted value based on an online valuation source rather than a formal appraisal, instead of "Current FMV *TBD," we might include "Current FMV as of 1/1/2026: $1,100,000 based on compromise agreements (1/1/2026 Zillow value $1,050,000)." While this detail does not constitute a formalized agreement between the parties, it does reflect both parties' estimated value of the asset and the basis of the value, ensuring any separate consulting professionals have the same information as the clients.

The purpose of mediator-prepared financial disclosures is to streamline the financial disclosure process, to prevent the need for duplicate efforts whenever possible, and to ensure that all details that may be needed in the mediation or formal agreement are included in the financial disclosures at the start of the case. Otherwise, the mediator or the parties may need to pause the mediation to hunt through statements and websites for information that could have been pulled into the financial disclosures to begin with for easy access and use during the mediation discussions. Such mid-meeting hunting slows down the progress and momentum in each mediation session.

For example, there may be different options available in assigning real property with a mortgage if the home loan is in both parties' names or just in one party's name. That information should be clear in the financial disclosures. We frequently encounter clients who are not certain how their real estate is titled or whose name is on the loan. They come to realize the importance of this information when we discuss whether the mortgage needs to be refinanced or assumed if one party will be keeping the home, or whether a simple title transfer or multiple transfers may be needed if the home is titled in the name of the marital trust or just in the clients' names as individuals. The hurdles that may need to be overcome for one party to keep the home instead of a sale or co-ownership can impact the viability of the options being discussed. Having all the information up front ensures the requirements associated with each option can be thoroughly explored and helps to avoid misunderstandings when either client makes assumptions about how their assets are titled or what steps would be needed to make changes.

As another example regarding retirement assets, the options and costs for tracing separate interests, valuing the assets, or transferring such assets pursuant to divorce are different for a defined benefit pension plan or a defined contribution savings plan, or for a 401(k) versus an IRA. And of course, the tax implications for a pretax 401(k) are different from a posttax Roth IRA. However, we frequently receive financial disclosures reflecting "Charlie's IRA—$252,222," which turns out to be a 401(k) or 403(b) and not an IRA at all. Or we see "Sam's Adobe retirement—$151,345," which tells us nothing about the account type, how we might need to consider valuing the account, or the options available for dividing the account.

It is critical to include the account statements and to identify the details for each account. If the statements are reviewed in preparing the disclosures, it would become clear that "Charlie's IRA" should actually be "Charlie's Visa Inc. 401(k) held with Vanguard (plan no. *8888); account balance as of 12/31/2024: $252,222 less $52,250 loan balance (net value $199,972)." And that "Sam's Adobe retirement" should be "Sam's Adobe Inc. 401(k) held with Fidelity (plan no. *1212); account balance as of 3/31/2025: $151,345 TBD if Sam also has a separate TSP plan with Adobe." If these turned out to be defined benefit pension plans instead of 401(k)s, different valuations, source documents, and division options would need to be discussed in mediation.

Including the account details and balances that match the statements provided in the financial disclosures at the outset of the case is crucial for efficient discussions in mediation. Based on their mediation experience, the mediator knows what information will be important in the discussion and can ensure such details are included in the financial disclosures to eliminate the need for mid-mediation hunting parties, which slow down progress and increase costs and frustration due to lack of transparency at the outset or lack of progress in mediation due to these diversions.

Another option many mediators prefer is for the clients to work with a neutral financial professional for the sole purpose of gathering source documents and completing the draft financial disclosures for the parties. This option works when there is well-integrated communication between the mediator and financial professional to coordinate on drafts and details together.

B. Mediating with Disclosures Prepared by Clients or Counsel

When financial disclosures have been exchanged prior to the start of mediation, the mediator will need to determine the most efficient strategy for managing any incomplete or inconsistent disclosures from the parties or counsel. While mediating settlement discussions with incomplete financial details is possible, it slows down the progress and can lead to additional professional time searching for details or unraveling inconsistencies.

Separate attorneys often try to minimize professional fees at the outset for their settlement-oriented clients and are focused on getting settlement discussions started with "preliminary financial disclosures" that do not include account details or statements that will be needed in the mediation. Without the last four digits of the account numbers or knowing which accounts are joint and which ones are held in separate names, it can be confusing to know which account is being discussed in the meeting, which can be frustrating for clients and slow down progress. These details impact the sense of transparency as well as the options available to the parties in their settlement discussions and should be available from the outset and not a detail to add in later. What was intended as a time-saving strategy has the opposite effect; significant gaps in information that go unchecked in the financial disclosures slow down mediation progress.

As family law professionals, we know there are distinct requirements and options available to the clients depending on the type of retirement asset. And attorneys are aware that disclosures with significant gaps in basic information are not useful and can work to include more detail to help their clients work through the settlement issues in their cases. For example, instead of "401(k) $120,000," which is really a rollover IRA from a prior 401(k), the attorney could reflect that as: "IRA with Vanguard (account *4321) held in Ryan's name (includes 401(k) rollover from 2010–2015 employment with Adobe, Inc.); balance as of 3/31/2025: $121,030." Even though there may be issues for further discussion and disclosure in the mediation, this initial level of detail provides the basic information needed to get the discussion started without significant omissions.

As another example, we often see separate disclosures that reflect employee equity, such as "RSUs $150,000." As family law professionals, we know this is an incomplete picture. This fails to identify the issuer of the restricted stock, the holding institution, and vesting status. Self-represented clients may take a first pass at their own list of assets and liabilities, but additional detail is needed to begin discussing these issues in mediation. Separate attorneys can help their clients by ensuring these details are provided up front, which will help move the settlement discussions forward more efficiently.

When separate disclosures are prepared by clients or counsel, if the account details are missing (i.e., account numbers, institutions, account holder names) or if only screenshots or incomplete statements are provided, it can be time consuming to reconcile the two sets of disclosures. Common questions when incomplete disclosures have been provided might be any of the following: "Are there four retirement accounts or three? Are these accounts the same as the accounts the other party identified? Are these joint accounts or separately titled accounts? Are any of these assets held in a joint or separate trust? What type of employee equity or private equity is this? Is it vested or unvested? What is the structure of this interest?" Needing to ask any of these questions during settlement negotiations takes the focus off brainstorming settlement options and places everyone back into the information-gathering stage of the case, which can make it feel like the case is dragging rather than feeling progress is being made. Similarly, mediators who draft marital settlement agreements often end up spending far more time than would otherwise be needed as a result of insufficient detail or inconsistencies in each party's financial disclosures that are not easily reconciled due to missing information.

These issues underscore the importance of obtaining and organizing all the financial details for both parties as soon as possible in the mediation so this does not delay the parties having productive discussions and reaching complete agreements. Even if complete agreements are reached, lack of details in the client or counsel-prepared financial disclosures can delay the parties being able to sign their formal agreements since key details needed to formalize enforceable agreement are missing. Losing momentum in the settlement discussions or in the drafting process due to missing information that could have been obtained earlier in the case is a missed opportunity for efficiently guiding the parties to the signing stage of their formal agreements.

If the separate attorneys prefer to prepare their own client's financial disclosures, and if there are substantial information gaps or inconsistencies, it can save considerable time in the overall process for the attorneys to meet to compare and clarify their lists of assets and any open questions before the disclosures are signed and exchanged. The separate attorneys know—just as the mediator knows—how important the asset and debt details are in formalizing enforceable agreements, and the mediator can request that the attorneys meet to fill in any gaps in the disclosures if that appears to be the most efficient process. Other times, the mediator may recognize the need to just work through the information-gathering process with the clients directly. In mediation, this can take the form of informal supplementation of the parties' formal disclosures, or the circumstances may call for formal augmentation of each party's financial disclosures, which can be discussed with the clients or attorneys involved.

There are also cases in which the clients are extremely cost sensitive and prefer to prepare their own financial disclosures. For all the reasons just noted, we discourage this due to the additional professional time needed on the back end in drafting agreements based on disclosures prepared by someone other than a family law professional. However, in cases with straightforward assets or those with fewer accounts in general, the mediator can simply guide the clients to add the detail that is needed so it is available in the next mediation and in the drafting of the formal agreements. The mediator might say:

> It is very important that we have all the account details in your financial disclosures, and I know how important it is for you to minimize professional fees. Do you both want to go back and add in the institution, account type, last four digits of the account number, whose name each account is in, and the balance and date that matches the statement you are providing so we have this for our next mediation? The alternative is to provide us the statements and we will do a detailed review so we can update your disclosures, but this could be more expensive.

Regardless of whether the disclosures are prepared by counsel, clients, or mediator, the mediator should always ensure any required declarations related to the financial disclosures have been executed and filed with the court prior to the judgment submission; missing declarations can result in rejection of the judgment, leading to delays in court processing and finalization of the court case.

C. Advantages of Working Settlement Spreadsheets

In many cases, particularly those in which the parties have already exchanged financial disclosures prior to mediation, the mediator may want to prepare their own working settlement spreadsheet or marital balance sheet to combine (and conform) the available information for all assets. This work ensures the mediator has consistent asset and liability details for settlement discussions and ensures the information needed for the formal agreements is available and does not slow down the drafting process once agreements are reached. Even in cases in which our office has prepared the disclosures, we often copy in the detail from the formal list of assets and liabilities into a more usable, modifiable, working spreadsheet for purposes of the settlement discussion.

The mediator can share their working settlement spreadsheet with the parties and counsel and any other professionals involved in the case. This ensures everyone on the team is working with the same information and any clarifications or updates can be made in the context of the mediation.

When neutral forensic accountants or other neutral financial professionals are involved, the financial professional may take the lead on creating and updating the marital balance sheet for settlement discussions. The mediator can collaborate with the financial professional to ensure the spreadsheet reflects the information needed in the discussions and formal agreements. In those cases, the mediator can call or meet with the financial professional to discuss the structure of the spreadsheet to maximize its utility during mediation for both professionals. This can typically be done most easily prior to the financial professional sharing the first version of the marital balance sheet. Since that is not always possible, the mediator should feel comfortable to contact the financial professional to talk through options, since both professionals are neutral and if they are not fully co-mediating the case, they are both in the role of helping both clients work through the settlement issues together and resolving their case as efficiently as possible. An example might be: "Thank you for all the work you've put into creating the marital balance sheet. I'd like to figure out the best way to get the information you need and the information I need into this. Can we look at this together and figure out what could work for both of us?" Respectful collaboration like this between professionals benefits the clients and all the professionals in the case.

As a hands-on mediator, I always want to make sure settlement frameworks and calculations are clear and understandable to both parties. This means that even in cases with comprehensive financial disclosures, it still may be helpful to have a separate working spreadsheet with settlement calculations. These working spreadsheets might include just the condensed information needed for the settlement discussions and not all the details we would include in the formal disclosures. This typically includes all assets and liabilities, or it might include limited issues depending on the settlement discussions. For example, we might have a separate section that only includes the real estate division and the retirement division if those are the core issues for the parties who want to see how those items stack up against each other. Or it might include a global settlement summary, including the division of assets, a support buyout, reimbursements between the parties, and contribution to professional fees. Or calculations might just be needed to track the reconciliation of reimbursements against asset equalizations.

Whether or not a more comprehensive balance sheet or working settlement spreadsheet exists, I often create rough calculations with basic formulas for adding, subtracting, multiplying, or dividing during mediation just to show the clients or counsel the logic I am seeing or to help clarify what they are trying to convey. Talking about an issue can be different from seeing it reflected in a short, uncomplicated settlement calculation on everyone's screen or on a whiteboard.

For example, one party might have a framework of issues they are conceptualizing, and I can see the other party isn't following. In this case, I might say: "Let me put these numbers into a quick spreadsheet calculation I can share with both of you on the screen just so we know what Devon is proposing. Does that work for both of you?" I might include shorthand labels and headings, but if anything remains unclear, I can fill in more detail just to make the calculations clearer. I generally include a cleaned-up version of our rough calculations with the clients afterward in the "Next Steps" section of my follow-up email.

The mediator should keep in mind that not everyone is a fan of spreadsheets—maybe the mediator isn't even a fan of spreadsheets! But their utility in mediation is hard to deny. I have often been in meetings with clients or professionals who declare themselves not to be spreadsheet fans only to have those same individuals remark on how clear the structure became just being able to see the notes and calculations in a simple spreadsheet with clear labels and headings in our meeting. The goal is to minimize the amount of information and details for the clients to read while balancing the need for useful information. In other words, less is more with these impromptu calculations.

With the more comprehensive settlement spreadsheets, it can be helpful to check in with the professionals and clients to ask if there are any proposed changes that would make this more useful for the settlement discussions. The purpose of the comprehensive working settlement spreadsheet is to assist the mediator as well as the clients and professionals to identify the information available, to flag information still needed, to indicate areas of agreement and areas that still need to be addressed, and to see all of this in a single detailed snapshot. There may be additional spreadsheet tabs that become necessary or helpful in a mediation, such as a separate retirement offset calculation tab or a separate support tab, and those can be easily added at any time throughout the mediation. The work our office does to create comprehensive settlement spreadsheets is typically done outside of mediation sessions, but updates can be made (and saved) during the mediation when appropriate. Other times, the mediator may just highlight certain areas of the spreadsheet during mediation to revisit after mediation when additional focus and concentration can be devoted or have someone with more sophisticated spreadsheet capabilities jump in to assist.

While some cases benefit from impromptu calculations during a mediation session and other cases require more comprehensive settlement calculations, there are other cases in which there is little to no benefit to creating a working spreadsheet of any kind. Instead, bullet points or numbered lists may be the clearest way to summarize and outline the issues being discussed and proposed in those cases.

As with any tools available to the mediator, there are no right or wrong methods of approaching, structuring, or reflecting options, issues, proposals, or tentative agreements throughout the process. However the framework of issues and agreements is structured, it should be useful for the clients and professionals, helping to organize and manage the issues in the case with the goal of moving the case and clients efficiently forward toward completion of their case.

7

Case Management in Mediation Sessions

Every action the mediator takes needs to be in furtherance of the clients' goals of reaching the conclusion of their case. With this in mind, the mediator schedules meetings as needed, reschedules meetings if the clients or professionals are not ready, and keeps an eye on all the moving parts to continue to move the case forward. And each mediation provides an opportunity for neutral case management by the mediator.

A. Setting the Stage for Each Meeting

Starting each meeting by briefly talking about the structure of the meeting and what to expect can be grounding and calming for everyone involved. Grounding happens by focusing on the process and present moment which can help minimize anxiety so everyone can access the problem-solving parts of their brains.

Mapping out the structure might include the length of the mediation session, confirming there are no time conflicts, and discussing the format for the meeting. The format discussion can include whether the meeting will be a joint session throughout or whether there is a plan to meet separately. In addition, it is helpful for clients to understand what to expect at the end of the meeting and any follow-up involved for the parties and the mediator.

At the outset of each meeting, the mediator should also identify the primary purpose of the mediation, whether there is an expectation that agreements on temporary or more global substantive issues may be made in the session, or whether the meeting is more of a case management meeting needed to identify issues, gather information, and/or create a plan together for the next steps. Effectively managing expectations starts with setting a plan for the meeting, working through the plan during the meeting, and then wrapping up the meeting by summarizing what occurred and what will happen next.

Here are a few examples of how the mediator might start with the schedule and structure (i.e., after any introductions that may be needed):

- "It's 10:00 now and we are scheduled until 12:00 today. Our plan is for the three of us to meet jointly so we can get through the information gathering we've already started, but if we need to hop into separate rooms for any reason, that's an option as well. Are there are any time constraints we should be aware of for anyone?"
- "We scheduled this as a joint meeting at our last mediation; based on the emails I received over the last couple of days, I would like to briefly meet with each of you separately. So in a few minutes, once we talk about our goals for today and what to expect, I will meet first with Robin for 15 minutes and then with Sue for 15 minutes before we meet back here jointly at 9:30 until 10:30 when we are scheduled to end today. Do you have any questions or does this plan work for both of you?"
- "We are scheduled for a quick case management meeting today. I blocked off 30 minutes for this meeting but we might not need that much time based on the short agenda we have. Does that sound right to the two of you?"

And here are some examples of what might follow that schedule and structure introduction to identify what to expect at the end of the meeting. This also helps clients (and professionals) to know they won't need to take copious notes on their action items since the mediator has let them know at the outset that the mediator will track and share these items with the team after the meeting:

- "At the end of our meeting today, we will work on scheduling our next mediation and recap everyone's action items, which I will send out by email as well."
- "At the end of our meeting, we can identify the decisions that still need to be made, and we can agree on a timeline for those decisions. I will send an email with the agreed follow-up steps."
- "At the end of our meeting today, we will decide together what action items might make sense depending on how far we get today—and we can talk about what the remaining steps of your case are and when you can expect a draft agreement depending on where we are in our discussions."
- "Our plan for today is to work through the remaining open issues in your Mediation Summary so I can start drafting your formal agreements. I know you are both hoping to have your formal agreements signed by the end of the month, which is feasible from my end as long as we close out any of those open cleanup items today. I will update the

Mediation Summary as we resolve each item so I can send it out to you after our meeting today before we start drafting the formal agreement. Does that sound like a good plan?"

In addition, for an initial mediation in which the mediator is meeting with the clients for the first time, the mediator can ensure the parties understand the mediator's neutral role and the confidentiality of mediation (which is likely just a reminder of what is already in the Agreement to Mediate). If the mediator is meeting with parties and counsel separately for the first time, the mediator can let the parties and counsel know how confidential information will be treated in the mediation.

Before we get too far into action items and agendas, we should check in with our clients. As mediators, we are always balancing the emotional and psychological needs of both clients in addition to guiding them efficiently through a complex and often overwhelming process. This means that we are working to ground everyone by managing their expectations for the meeting and follow-up and also checking in to see how all of this is landing with each client. Before we rush headlong into agendas, we should consider what each client may need emotionally as they are starting out in this process or in the meeting. Something like the following might make sense: "Before we get into the open issues on our agenda today, I would like to take a few minutes to see how you're feeling coming into this meeting [or to find out how things have been going since our last meeting]." Or the mediator might take the opportunity to discuss each client's goals and interests or to remind the clients of what their stated goals were in the last mediation or any ground rules that feel important to reiterate. These are essential mediator tools that don't need to be detailed here, but should not be forgotten in the quest for efficient case management.

Once these preliminary but necessary foundational steps are completed in the meeting, the next step should be a quick runthrough of the meeting agenda, which may also have been shared when the meeting was scheduled to avoid surprises and encourage preparedness by the parties or counsel. A quick overview of the agenda at the start of the mediation helps to set expectations in the context of the time set aside for the meeting and what is realistic to achieve in that meeting.

After listing the items on the agenda, the mediator can ask the participants if there are any additional items to add to the agenda or whether the mediator's agenda includes the issues they are each hoping to discuss. It is important to keep this runthrough of (or additions to) the agenda a high-level overview so the brief agenda discussion does not get hijacked by diving into the substance of each item prematurely or out of logical sequence. If a party or professional brings too much detail into the agenda overview, the mediator can remind everyone: "This is just an overview of the agenda so everyone knows what will be discussed—the details of each agenda item can be discussed when we get to that issue." This is one way of keeping meeting participants on track, whether clients or professionals. The mediator should communicate the agenda and discuss any input respectfully, professionally, and without defensiveness, because the mediator is the team leader and should lead by example at all times.

As team leader, the mediator typically sets the order of the agenda. Remember, the parties do not know how all the issues are going to be addressed and resolved, what might be interrelated, or what a logical sequence might be. As so many of our clients say, "We don't know what we don't know!" However, it can be helpful to ask if either party has an issue they would like to prioritize since this can be a useful data point for the mediator, who can then determine how best to manage the parties' respective priorities.

As mediators, we strive to maintain balance between empowering the parties to be the decision makers in their own case with the need for the mediator to maintain control of the process to help the parties make progress in a productive manner. If the mediator starts each mediation asking the parties what they want to tackle first, or what they want to discuss, that can tip this balance to the point that the parties do not feel the mediator is in control and undermines their confidence that the mediator can effectively guide them through a process the parties may struggle to understand. There have been numerous times in which I was engaged as the second mediator to work with the parties, with the most common complaints being that the first mediator did not set agendas, that topics and discussions were dictated by the parties and not the mediator, or that each discussion was just a free-flow conversation without an agenda. Other common complaints are that previous mediators did not document agreements made in the meetings. Such clients are often referred to me by other family law professionals who are familiar with my agenda-oriented case management style and the importance I place on empowering clients while maintaining control of the process. These can be critical hallmarks to a successful mediation in complex family law cases.

Once the schedule and structure have been set at the start of the mediation session, the mediator can let the parties know the order in which each agenda item will be addressed, unless there is something either client feels should be reprioritized.

- Ordering the agenda might happen organically, such as: "Our first agenda item will be to discuss the upcoming status conference with the court; then the documents and information still needed for the financial disclosures; and then we can get into the expense and budget details that you have started working on. Once we have those three items handled, we can discuss the stock option analysis and what else might be needed for our discussion next time on the retirement and brokerage accounts. We should have enough time to get through these agenda items in the 90 minutes we have scheduled today. Is there anything else you want to add to our radar either for today or next time?"

- Or the agenda might just be a quick list without the need for a specific order, such as: "I have four items on our agenda today, which are (1) finalize your agreements on the retirement division, (2) discuss options for the division of your private investments, (3) discuss the equity division, and (4) discuss reimbursements for the three-month period since separation. Does that order work for both of you and are there are any other agenda items you want to add in case we get through all of this in the next hour and a half?"

Typically, the mediator's expertise and intuition in considering and ordering the open issues for discussion will be accepted by the parties and counsel, which means everyone is ready to proceed based on the mediator's agenda.

Experienced mediators often recognize that certain issues may be more sensitive or triggering, and that more progress can be made if agreements on certain issues are handled first. Depending on the case, there might be benefits for the parties in resolving smaller or easier issues first to help gain momentum in a positive direction or to gain the parties' confidence by reaching agreements and limiting the scope of what still needs to be resolved. In other cases, smaller, less-fraught issues distract from the core issues, and the first issues to tackle in those cases may just be the largest and most complicated (though the mediator can still find other smaller paths to progress or "wins" in those situations that can also help to create positive momentum along the way).

The mediator needs to rely on their understanding of the parties and their specific needs and personalities to know how to prioritize the agenda items and then to work to keep everyone on track toward resolving those issues. And, of course, at times, agenda items may need to be moved around or issues added to the agenda—often due to events occurring outside the mediation—and the mediator can make necessary adjustments without rigidity but balancing being reasonable, efficient, productive, and mindful of the clients' needs as well as the feasibility of what can be accomplished within the time and structure of the meeting.

There may be occasions in which the discussion does not reach all the agenda items. Well before the end of the mediation session, the mediator can notify the parties of the remaining timing and agenda items not yet discussed to give the option of shifting to the other agenda topics. At the end of the mediation, the mediator can identify the agenda items that were not discussed so there is no concern that something was overlooked. The mediator can transparently address this with the following: "Our agenda today may have been too ambitious for the time reserved since we were unable to get to issue X and issue Y, which I know are both important issues for you. We are scheduled to meet again in three weeks, and we can either include these at the top of our agenda for next time or we can schedule a separate session in between just to focus on these two issues. What is your preference?" The mediator should also consider what is realistic for each set of clients in setting the agenda for the next mediation based on these experiences.

B. Making a Plan for the Start and End of the Case

Family law mediations can start before there are any court filings or at any point between the initiation of the court case until entry of final judgment or even beyond when postjudgment issues arise. Whether or not the court case has been initiated prior to the engagement of the mediator, the mediator can still work with the parties to plan the steps for starting the court case and the timing for finalizing their case as one of the first steps toward empowering the clients to be the decision makers in their own case. The mediator is in the unique position of being able to talk through these issues and help each party hear the other party's perspective and create the plan together at the outset. Knowing there is a plan on these issues can help reduce some of the anxiety the clients might feel about the uncertainties in their lives at this stage.

If the parties or their counsel have not yet started the court case, the mediator can create the plan with the parties for preparing, filing, and serving the petition and response for dissolution, discussing minimum waiting periods, what the steps at the end of the case look like with the court, and thinking generally about the timeline for finalizing their divorce. This helps focus the clients on the end goal and allows them to almost visualize being at that stage.

To start with, deciding whose name comes first in the court pleadings (typically referred to as the petitioner or the respondent) can be a joint decision. While legally insignificant in most jurisdictions, there are emotional factors as well as matters of convenience to consider. Discussing and making a plan for the filing and service together can minimize surprises and inconveniences. For example, a surprise service of a divorce petition at work or being served personally during a social or family gathering can undermine trust in the overall divorce process and erode any remaining good will between the clients and can easily be avoided with a coordinated plan. Other inconveniences that create unnecessary delays at the outset of a case, such as sending the petition to a party who will be traveling for two months, can also be avoided with a coordinated plan, including the option of swapping the petitioner and respondent roles.

The mediator can discuss the required court forms with the parties and share copies of the forms if desired so they can get comfortable with the layout of the forms and the court requirements. Some clients prefer this approach while others prefer to only briefly discuss the procedural issues in mediation and review the documents on their own afterward. The mediator can review with the clients the information needed, discuss options, and ensure neither client is advantaged over the other even at this stage of the process, including what is and is not being requested in the petition and response.

Once decisions have been made about the case initiation filings, the formal documents can be completed outside of the mediation session and sent for the clients' review and approval. This structure allows the clients to get a preview of the court documents and to know what to expect when they receive the completed forms, and it provides space for each client to review the documents after the meeting and to ask any follow-up questions.

Certain questions can be answered by the mediator and agreements or compromises can be reached in mediation on issues contained in the initial filings, including the date of separation or issues regarding support or child custody, for example. However, if either party needs legal advice, the mediator can encourage the clients to consult with their own separate attorneys before approving the case initiation documents. This can be tricky to navigate if either client has a litigation-oriented attorney who encourages an adversarial approach even at the initial filing stage.

For example, clients who agree to mediate and schedule their first mediation with the selected mediator can be thrown for a psychological loop if one of the parties' attorneys advises getting the petition filed and served the day before the first mediation session. I like to believe that most family law attorneys would not stage a surprise service of divorce papers the day before the first mediation, recognizing the negative impact this could have on the entire mediation process. And yet, this has certainly occurred in several of our cases but is incredibly counterproductive from the point of view of a neutral mediator.

As another example of litigation-focused counsel ignoring the impact of their actions on the entire mediation process, I have also encountered consulting attorneys advising their clients to make significant changes to neutral mediation-focused petition and response filings in which all rights are reserved. I have had attorneys advise clients that: "If the case falls out of mediation, we would need to file an amended Petition on X, Y, or Z issue and therefore we should push for changes to the petition [or response] now." A common example of this is indicating a request to terminate spousal support for the other party rather than a more neutral "TBD" for discussion in mediation.

Because an amended petition or response is one of the easier procedural steps to take in the event the mediation is not successful, I would encourage betting on the mediation being successful and not urging adversarial positions at the outset of mediation, given that there is no downside risk if mediation is not successful. But there is a downside risk to arguing legal positions before the clients have had the chance to work together in mediation, since that sets the tone for an adversarial mediation. It ensures both parties will act and react more defensively as well as offensively throughout what could otherwise be a nonadversarial process.

My guidance to attorneys is that they can be most helpful to the success of the mediation process their clients have chosen if they can be less litigation oriented. The clients are not "trying mediation"—they are "engaged in mediation." And our job as the professionals hired to assist them in this process—whether engaged as neutrals or separate professionals—is to support them and the success of the mediation from the outset of the case to achieve their goals.

Even at this early stage of discussing the initiation of the case, the mediator can also begin discussing options for finalizing the divorce and creating a plan for terminating marital status. It can be helpful to discuss family health insurance and tax filing up front to ensure there are no unilateral actions regarding these issues and to allow for options to be explored before the decision on when to finalize the divorce needs to be made.

The mediator can also open a discussion on any emotional or symbolic issues that may be important to the parties or their families in initiating their court case and considering options for finalizing their divorce. These discussions often cannot happen when separate attorneys are working in parallel or in court simply because the opportunity to jointly explore these issues does not naturally occur. But in mediation, the mediator can facilitate discussions on these potentially sensitive issues to understand each party's considerations and preferences on the timeline for their case without derailing the rest of the discussion.

C. Discussing Next Steps

The mediator should allow at least ten minutes at the end of each meeting to review the promised recap and discuss next steps, including the next meeting and agenda. Throughout the meeting, the mediator can keep track of all next steps and action items at the end of their mediation notes. This minimizes the time needed at the end of the meeting to sort through the notes and organize all the action items and ensures no details are missed.

For example, during the mediation, one party may indicate they will provide a response to a request or will supply a specific financial statement later that week. The mediator can add in their notes: "Alex will share Visa credit card statements for March 2024 through March 2025 with the group by end of this week, April 18th." This detail should be included in the body of the mediation notes where the discussion occurs so the notes and chronology of the discussion are clear for the mediator, but the mediator should also copy that language and paste it at the end of the day's mediation notes in a separate section titled "Next Steps" where all such things are tracked. The mediator can then jump back to the body of the mediation notes to continue the conversation. At the end of the meeting, all action items will be safely tucked into the Next Steps section for the mediator to read through, get everyone's agreement on the next steps, and send out by email following the meeting.

It may take a little practice to jump to the end of the notes mid-discussion (and there are keyboard shortcuts to help with this), but it is such an important tool to help manage all the follow-up steps that are discussed, whether in short or longer meetings, and ensure nothing gets missed. Another option is to highlight in a specific color all follow-up items throughout the mediation and then scroll back through the notes and read out the highlighted items at the end of the meeting, though this is a less-cohesive option and requires more work to create a list of next steps later. And other mediators may not take detailed notes other than agreements and follow-up steps and may just focus on keeping their Next Steps section up to date throughout the meeting.

There is nothing wrong with pausing in the mediation to say: "Let me just add this to our follow-up section and then we can move on." An alternative to build confidence or celebrate small wins might be: "This is great progress—let me just make a note about this agreement since I'll be sending a follow-up email and don't want to leave this out." Or whatever else feels appropriate in the moment.

Part of the recap of next steps should be identifying or scheduling the next meetings. In the Next Steps section of my notes, I either include the date and time of the next meeting so it's readily available, or I include a placeholder as a reminder that we need to schedule the next meeting.

It is important to consider each client's emotional stamina and information saturation points in scheduling follow-up mediations. My own preference is a 90-minute mediation since that typically provides time to get through numerous procedural and legal issues, reach tentative agreements on various settlement issues, and decide what to tackle next. In my experience, an hour and a half to two hours is enough to make substantial progress without overwhelming the parties and their capacity to consider so much information. That said, the length of each meeting will always depend on who will be attending, whether the mediator is meeting with everyone jointly or separately, and the purpose of the meeting and number of issues on the agenda.

A case management meeting with counsel (as discussed in the next chapter) might be scheduled for 30 to 60 minutes, while a case management meeting with clients and counsel may need to be 60 to 90 minutes depending on the agenda. In cases without representing counsel, if one or both parties seem overwhelmed by the length of the meetings, the mediator might ask: "Do you prefer to schedule our next meeting for just an hour with a more limited agenda or do you prefer to schedule a longer meeting to push through these five open issues?" If there is a difference of opinions or processing speeds, the mediator may not be able to pose such open-ended questions and instead might make a suggestion such as: "I want to ensure we are having the most productive meetings possible and would like to suggest that we schedule our next mediation for one hour with the following agenda items. . . . Does that work for both of you?"

D. Variations in Mediator Notetaking

As noted earlier, notetaking styles vary between practitioners and there is no single right or wrong method for tracking what needs to be tracked. One of the most impressive civil mediators I shadowed in San Francisco very early in my mediation career, Harris Weinberg, was both graceful and methodical in his mediation notetaking. He would pause to let an idea circulate or a proposal sink in while he carefully made his handwritten notes about what was occurring in the mediation. At first, that notetaking time made me feel anxious, imagining everyone watching him write notes like a therapist keeping track of secret thoughts. But then I realized that how he timed his notetaking, what he said about his notetaking as it was happening, were all part of his particular style of very effective and thoughtful mediation.

Like Harris Weinberg, I use my notetaking to organize my thoughts, flag issues to follow up on in the mediation, and track next steps throughout the mediation. However, because I happen to type quickly, my notes tend to be a blend of untrained stenography with my own shorthand such as *DOM* for date of marriage, *DOS* for date of separation, as well as *pre-m*, *during-m*, *post-sep*, *jdx* for jurisdiction, *H* for husband, *W* for wife, *M* and *D* for unmarried mom and dad, and first initials for same-sex partners such as *Y* and *M*, or *HL* and *VV* for attorney or other professional initials, as well as my own initials *PML* when I want to indicate what suggestion I might have made to distinguish from a proposal suggested by a party or counsel. This results in my notes being a close approximation of a verbatim record of the meeting even though I am talking and typing at the same time, which helps me organize my thoughts and notice gaps or flag follow-up issues

In preparation for each mediation, I open my notes file to get organized for the meeting. My notes file is an ongoing Word document that has all the case and contact information at the beginning and includes a chronology of events as they occur, starting with the first contact with our office and with the most recent events at the end of the document. The "old school" version of this would be a single legal pad used for each case in which each entry is added as it occurs, with the date included so the chronology is clear when the notes need to be consulted. The "newer school" version of this would be any number of available AI notetaking applications, which the mediator would need to carefully vet and edit to ensure reliability as well as confidentiality, which I am not convinced exists yet for our unique purposes.

I start each meeting entry by adding the date, who will be participating in the meeting, whether we are meeting in person or via video, what the scheduled start and end times are, and when the last meeting was. I also create sections I anticipate we will be working on so I can just start typing as the conversation occurs. This starts with an "Agenda" section; the discussion topics section, which I label based on the discussion such as "Goals/Interests," "Income/Support," "123 House Street," "Private Investments," "Professional Fees," and so on. And I always create my Next Steps section at the end of the notes at the outset so that section is ready for me to drop details in as action items are discussed. In the Next Steps section, I include any additional meetings that may already be scheduled, and below all of this, I include the scheduled end time for the mediation so I don't lose track of time. Once the meeting concludes, I include the actual end time in my notes, which helps for billing purposes, but also helps to track any patterns in meeting duration. For example, if we schedule an hour and a half but always need two hours in a case or only use one hour, that can help in scheduling follow-up meetings and setting expectations.

If I am meeting separately with parties and counsel at any time during the meeting, I make a heading for that with start and end times, so I can also be mindful of how much time I've spent with each side and keep myself and everyone else on track with timing. It can also be helpful to set a timer on a phone or watch including a sound so the mediator and other participants can hear and comply with expectations that each separate meeting will be ~30 minutes, for example.

I also tend to use other shortcuts or flags in my notes such as highlighting in a certain color (usually yellow) for agreements and highlighting in a different, more obnoxious color (such as bright orange or green) for issues I'm flagging to make sure we come back to address or questions during the meeting. I might also use single and double asterisks for certain issues, quotes to indicate a particularly interesting direct quote, or parentheses to reflect a thought or reaction I might have to something said or a particularly emotional reaction from a client.

As an example of a different type of notetaker, my mediation partner Shelley Kennedy, while also a fast typist, does not keep verbatim notes during mediation since she feels it takes away from her focus on the parties in the mediation. Instead, after each meeting, she performs what I call a "data dump" and either prepares her detailed notes at that time or uses the speech-to-text function of her computer to "download" the details of the conversation and edits those notes for clarity. She also happens to have a great ability to recall detailed information, so this type of postmediation data dump works well for her, whereas that might not be a great option for someone else, myself included. In other words, there is no single right or wrong approach, other than clearly keeping track of key discussion points and next steps for everyone.

In Chapter 9, we will discuss options for sending follow-up information after each meeting. Just remember that the mediator is keeping track of everyone's action items and next steps and should be sharing those action items after each meeting to keep everyone on track. Keeping detailed notes is an important part of the necessary follow-up and is one of the most common complaints we hear about other mediators.

Also keep in mind that while most states have mediation confidentiality statutes that govern the admissibility of information and documents produced in mediation, via adoption of the Uniform Mediation Act (UMA) or other framework for confidentiality in mediation through legislation or caselaw, levels of protection vary from state to state. In California, mediator notes and mediator testimony are inadmissible in any proceeding, which is intended to encourage openness in mediation. In other words, mediator notes are just a tool for the mediator's use during the mediation sessions, to help in mediation follow-up correspondence and mediation summaries, and to keep track of various discussions and topics throughout the mediation, but not to share directly with clients or counsel. I never share my mediator notes of course, but I certainly rely heavily on my notes in creating follow-up emails and mediation summaries to share with the mediation team.

Some of these case management tools can be useful in any type of meeting, not just family law mediations. In the following chapters, we will identify the specific stages of the family law case that can greatly benefit from neutral case management, including practical steps to ensure the mediator can most effectively and efficiently steer the clients and the professionals through each of these areas to a successful and organized outcome.

8

Case Management Conferences

A. The Benefit of Check-Ins with Professionals and Clients

Litigating counsel are likely familiar with the case management role of the court and what to expect at status conferences at court but may be less familiar with the case management role of mediators or the benefits of case management conferences (aka case management meetings) in mediation. However, mediators with strong organizational and respectful "herding" skills can be an asset to the parties as well as the separate attorneys and the court by identifying issues and concerns, resolving discovery issues, and keeping the case moving toward settlement. While case management meetings may not be needed in every case, the mediator should be on the lookout for signs from the parties or counsel that a more active case management role may be beneficial, including case management conferences.

The general purpose of the case management conference is to identify and agree on next steps and a timeline for each of those steps before the next case management meeting or mediation session. How the meetings are structured, and with whom, depends on whether the mediator is primarily working with just the parties or whether the other professionals have a more involved role.

It can be particularly helpful for the mediator to schedule case management meetings when counsel, forensic accountants, and other professionals are involved in the case. In these cases, the first case management meeting can be scheduled immediately upon the mediator's engagement. This initial case management meeting allows the mediator to get the lay of the land with other professionals who may have already been working the case, to find out more about the specific issues in the case or the issues standing in the way of settlement, and any other relevant case background details such as the parties' personal or financial histories. This also helps the mediator get a sense of the personalities of the professionals and discuss how they envision their own roles as well as the mediator's role and for the mediator to establish their role as the case manager simply by being there and managing the team, the agenda, the meeting, and the follow-up.

As the case progresses, the mediator can schedule additional case management meetings with the professionals to keep the case moving forward between mediation sessions by identifying action items and setting timelines, or discussing discrete discovery and settlement issues that may benefit from collaborative professional brainstorming. Action items discussed might include anything from a mediation briefing schedule, formal disclosure exchange dates, exchange of informal disclosures or exchanges for specific issues in the case, agreeing on a neutral forensic accountant and scope of their work, determining whether additional information such as appraisals or brokers' estimates might be useful, and agreeing on the professionals to engage and the timing of such engagements. Alternatively, the goal of the case management meeting might be limited to creating a plan for resolving threshold settlement issues that may impact many other issues, such as date of separation, and a plan for resolving the issues.

Case management conferences might be scheduled as video conferences or phone calls, though I prefer video conferencing so we can share screens with spreadsheets and other documents that might be helpful to share with the group. Case management meetings with professionals can be scheduled for 30 to 60 minutes depending on the agenda, and the mediator should send out the agenda when scheduling the meeting so counsel and any other professionals can be prepared to discuss the agenda items and ensure a productive meeting.

The mediator's role in these case management meetings is to lead the meeting, identify and agree on the agenda (or any items to add to the already set agenda), efficiently work through the agenda items, and ensure the discussion is collaborative and productive for the benefit of the shared clients.

Being efficient doesn't mean not being friendly or collegial, as these things are not mutually exclusive; in fact, a friendly rapport between professionals tends to lead to more efficient and productive discussions rather than detracting from such goals. This means the mediator and professionals should feel free to catch up as colleagues on travel, work, or family issues for a few minutes, particularly when waiting for the other professionals to arrive. The mediator should be mindful of the time and not let the friendly catching up extend more than a few minutes, which can easily be done with a gentle nudge by the mediator to say: "Well, we're all here now so let's go ahead and get into our agenda." Or if the collegial catching up feels like it's taking up—or threatening to take up—a bit too much time, the mediator can cut in and say something like: "I hate to derail such an entertaining part of our meeting but I know we have limited time today and a lot on our agenda. Are we ready to get started?" The mediator does not need to be the "fun police" since lively and friendly professional discussions support collaborative and productive working relationships. This does not need to be a harsh cutoff but rather a gentle nudge that maintains the same friendly tone that has been established and heads the ship in the right direction toward productively discussing the issues on the agenda. The other professionals know why they are at the meeting and have the same intention to get to work. It is the mediator's role to balance the desire to foster collegiality with the need to be productive, and the mediator will have plenty of opportunities to practice and refine their own version of this balancing act.

Just as the mediator does in every meeting, at the end of each case management meeting with the professionals, the mediator can read through the list of action items compiled throughout the meeting, ensuring each professional knows who has agreed to (or has been assigned to) do each action item and let the team know there will be a follow-up email with these action items. The mediator will also discuss and schedule the next meeting(s) with the professionals, which might be a case management follow-up meeting and/or a mediation session with clients and professionals.

To ensure the mediator has sufficient time at the end of each meeting to review action items and work on scheduling, the mediator should be sure to reserve at least the last ten minutes of each case management meeting for this wrap-up time.

The following is an example of how the mediator might recap the case management meeting with professionals (and which will be used for a more organized and detailed follow-up email to the group afterward):

> In the remaining few minutes, let's go through the next steps we've discussed today and which I will send out to everyone by email afterward:
>
> - I will send the updated settlement spreadsheet to the two of you today and you will each review this with your clients before our next mediation with clients.
> - Richard will finalize the stipulation on temporary issues this week based on our discussion today and share that with us with the goal of getting that signed by the end of next week.
> - You are both discussing with your clients options for appraising the real properties now or getting brokers' estimates.
> - Greg will share his client's stock plan documents before our next meeting so we can determine whether or not a time rule analysis is needed based on the agreed date of separation.

- Richard will share documentation before our next meeting on where his client's shares are held and whether there is any vesting or whether these were purchased or awarded outright.
- You are each going to discuss the status of the parties' division of household items so we can either cross this off our list or keep it on our radar for discussion.
- We tentatively scheduled our next mediation with clients and counsel for July 1st from 9:30 to 11:30 pending confirmation from the clients, which you are going to discuss with them and confirm with my office. Our agenda for that hour and a half meeting will be focused on information gathering in order to update and clarify any issues or questions in the settlement calculations spreadsheet and we can schedule a more in-depth mediation session at that time.

Is there anything else you have on your follow-up lists? If not, I'll go ahead and email these items out to each of you and you will share with the clients rather than me sending to the full group, is that right?

When separate attorneys are not directly involved in the mediation, it can still be helpful for the mediator to have shorter "check-in meetings" with the clients when the clients are doing the legwork on various steps before a substantive mediation session can be scheduled. Check-in meetings with clients are the same as case management meetings with professionals with the only difference being the use of a layperson's label for the meeting with clients. This labeling helps the clients know that the purpose is a check-in rather than a full mediation session in which substantive agreements might be reached, helping to manage everyone's expectations. On the other hand, calling for a regular mediation might lead one or both clients to anticipate negotiating on substantive issues in their overall settlement and could lead to frustration if the purpose of the meeting is solely to check in on the status of various steps such as the clients' document gathering for disclosures or to discuss engaging a home appraiser or forensic accountant.

As with case management meetings with professionals, the purpose of the check-in meeting with clients is to ensure the information both parties need to productively discuss the substantive issues and reach agreements is obtained and available on an agreed timeframe before the next mediation session. This might include walking the parties through the information-gathering stage of sharing documents for financial disclosures, checking on their informal exchange of account statements that may be needed for reimbursement issues, identifying appraisals that may be needed, determining what information might be needed regarding employee equity or private equity, discussing questions regarding interim issues or calculations, agreeing on a timeline and assignment of roles to keep these steps moving forward, or any other action items relevant to the settlement issues in the case.

Keeping client check-in meetings to 30 minutes with a set agenda emailed in advance helps manage both parties' expectations and minimizes anxiety about what might happen in the meeting, which ensures a more productive meeting. At the end of each check-in meeting, the mediator should reserve five to ten minutes to discuss follow-up actions and schedule the next meeting with the clients. The next meeting might be another check-in meeting or, if the information needed to discuss and reach agreements is expected to be available, a full mediation session with a broader agenda to include specific settlement issues can be scheduled for the appropriate meeting duration.

The following is an example of how the mediator might summarize the agreed next steps in a check-in meeting with clients, which will also be used for the quick follow-up email afterward:

> Before we sign off, let's just quickly recap the follow-up items discussed today and which I will email to you both afterward:
>
> - Mike will share his Q1 bonus paycheck in the next couple of days.
> - Alberto will share his most recent paycheck in the next couple of days.
> - My office will prepare the bonus support calculations by the end of next week.
> - You are both going to review the monthly and bonus support calculations with your separate attorneys before our next meeting.
> - You are going to exchange proposed holiday schedules a week before our next meeting so you have time to consider the other parent's requests.
> - We scheduled our next mediation to take place on September 5th from 10:00 to 11:30, and my office will send out the video conference details. We discussed your shared preference that our meeting structure continue with just the three of us and not bring the attorneys into the mediation at this time. Our agenda will be to discuss the overall structure for support and expense sharing and if we have time, we can also start discussing the retirement and investment account issues we flagged today.
>
> Does this sound like a good plan for now or is there anything else we need to add to the follow-up list or to our agenda for next time?

B. Follow Up to Manage Progress

Sending a follow-up email after each case management meeting or check-in meeting to clients, counsel, and any other professionals involved in the meeting is a critical component of case management and will be explored in further detail in the next chapter. For case management meetings and client check-ins, the follow-up should be relatively brief and sent the same day or the following day to maintain control of the flow of information and action items. If the mediator delays in this case management follow-up, bits and pieces might flow in from others about what they believe their action items or others' action items are or frame the discussion in a less-than-neutral manner. This can leave the mediator needing to clean up something that could have been more easily managed with the swift, comprehensive, and neutral follow-up email the same day or the day following the meeting, at the latest.

The mediator's case management follow-up correspondence should include each person's action items clearly itemized and timeframes for each action as well as the details and agenda for the next meeting. The mediator can track the completion of each action item and confirm all the specified action items have been completed to keep everyone on track in a helpful and collaborative manner.

Creating plans with parties and/or counsel and following up on action items helps to keep the case moving forward, and the mediator needs to watch for the possibility of a dropped or missing ball on the proverbial tennis court to make sure everyone knows what is happening next.

The follow-up email to counsel and other professionals might include the following:

- Sarah will discuss with her client the temporary support proposal from Kelly's 6/20/2025 email and report back to the group by the end of this week.
- Kelly will share her client's proposed division of household items by the end of this week.
- You will both discuss the proposed engagement of a neutral forensic accountant with your clients for purposes of the separate tracing issues and marital standard of living analysis so we can discuss this in our next meeting and initiate that process.
- Our next case management meeting is scheduled for November 1, 2025, from 9:15 to 10:15 a.m. and my office will send the link for our video conference.

In follow-up emails with unrepresented clients, the mediator might say: "I have included below the next steps from our meeting yesterday. . . . We discussed that it would be helpful to have each of these steps completed at least one week prior to our next meeting on August 25. I will check in with you both on August 18 to confirm we have received each of these items by then. Thank you both."

Memorializing the plan for each situation in a follow-up email ensures that parties and counsel know there is someone (i.e., the mediator) steering the ship and keeping track of what needs to happen and when. The mediator's goal is shepherding the clients and professionals to the next stage of reaching agreements together, which should always be everyone's shared goal.

9

Mediation Summaries and Other Critical Follow-Ups

As we have noted, every meeting should be followed by an email to manage the next steps for everyone involved, which is ideally sent out the same day as the meeting or the following day whenever possible. This follow-up can take the form of bullet points in an email or a more complete summary of the case, depending on the meeting. And each such follow-up email should be thought of as necessary case management for the parties, the mediator, and any other professionals who may be involved, whether directly in the meetings or in outside consulting roles.

If the mediator sends neutral follow-up correspondence just after the meeting, this lets the mediator set the neutral and collegial tone for the group and the email thread. This also prevents parties or clients from sending their own version of the case management plan, which might not be as comprehensive or as neutral as what the mediator would send.

Sending the follow-up email is an opportunity to effectively organize issues and action items for the benefit of everyone involved. Failing to send a follow-up email after the meeting detailing next steps can easily result in meeting participants not knowing what is needed or what is happening next even if next steps were discussed at the end of the meeting. This can be the result of inconsistent recollections by the parties or counsel, an oversaturation of information, a long emotional meeting, or the professionals needing to jump right into a meeting on a different case at the end of the meeting with the mediator. Whatever the reasons, not sending a clear follow-up email can result in one or both parties feeling lost and overwhelmed by a process that constantly threatens to devour them and can lead to the family law professionals feeling unsure that there is a cohesive plan.

In the worst case, lack of a clear plan outlined in an email following a meeting with clients could result in a client forgetting what they are supposed to be doing, feeling lost in an overwhelming process, or otherwise being unable to communicate the status of the case to their counsel. In turn, they may turn to their separate attorneys to escalate their involvement, which could lead to a more adversarial process. When separate consulting attorneys are not kept in the loop with status updates from the mediator following client-only mediations, the attorneys will try to get an understanding from their clients on the progress made and next steps; if the client doesn't know or cannot point to the mediator's follow-up email or more detailed mediation summary, the attorneys themselves may recommend escalation into litigation when they hear frustration from their clients or lack of a coherent plan to move the case forward.

A. Follow-Up Emails: Bullet Points to Keep Everyone on Track

The purpose of a follow-up email with bullet points is to clearly but concisely identify the issues discussed in each meeting, tentative agreements reached, agreed case management issues, action items (aka to-dos), and other next steps, including when or whether the next meeting is scheduled. This is best sent as soon as possible after the meeting since the details will be fresh in everyone's minds and will provide clients and counsel time to manage their own action items before the next meeting. My practice is to read through the Next Steps section in the meeting (as detailed in Chapter 7) to wrap up the session and note the end time for the mediation before starting my time for drafting my follow-up correspondence with the agreed next steps. Once I send the email correspondence, I note any dates for my legal assistant team to calendar, add any action items to my own to-do list, create my billing entries, and close the file so there are no loose ends.

Here is an example of a follow-up email from a case management meeting with counsel with bullet points to help organize the action items:

> Hi Michael and Beth:
>
> I have included below the next steps from our Case Management Conference today:
>
> - You both agree to complete and exchange your clients' financial disclosures by the end of next week [insert date here].
> - Beth is discussing Michael's request for Eric to advance the $5,000 retainer for the neutral forensic accountant for the marital standard of living analysis. Beth will let us know if this is agreeable via email by the end of this week [insert date here] so I can initiate the engagement with the neutral forensic. The goal is for the forensic accountant to complete their analysis by the end of next month, so

everyone has sufficient time to review and discuss the analysis with the forensic accountant at least three to four weeks prior to our full day mediation.

- Based on the steps above, we are tentatively holding all day Tuesday, October 1 at 9:30 a.m.–4:00 p.m. for our mediation with clients, counsel, and forensic accountants via Zoom. You will both confirm this date works for your clients and the forensic accountants in the next couple of days so we can confirm the date and share the video conference link.
- I will plan to schedule separate meetings with each of you and your clients so that preliminary settlement negotiations can take place before the joint mediation.

Please let me know if you have any questions or clarifications to the above. Otherwise, we will look forward to receiving the financial disclosures and hearing from both of you to confirm everyone's availability for mediation. Thank you.

Here is an example of a follow-up from a mediation with clients:

Hi Otis and Rafi:

Thank you both for a productive mediation today. I have included below the follow-up discussed today so we can continue your progress:

- You have tentatively agreed to use "$975,000 as the current value of the house and will consider options to sell or buyout on spouse's interest in the home at the end of your 6-month nesting period."
- Otis will provide the start and end dates you and the children lived in your last two family homes. Once we have this, we will complete the documents needed to start your court case.
- We will update your formal draft financial disclosures once we have the following documents you are each uploading to our Shared Folder using the Upload Link for Documents from Clients [insert hyperlinks here]:
    - Otis: Two vehicle titles, current unvested Zillow equity documentation, cost for current group health insurance (confirm if medical, dental, and vision) and breakdown by family member, which he will request from his benefits administrator.
    - Rafi: Current Fidelity brokerage statement, current Schwab IRA statement, private life insurance policy declarations (need document reflecting insurance company, death benefit, and beneficiary).
- Rafi will contact the health insurance broker now to discuss options for private coverage once your marital status is terminated: Meredith Rice-Bishop (https://ricebishopins.com/) (i.e., include contact information if this is a referral for the clients).

- You are working on detailing your monthly expenses so we can focus on the income, expenses, and support discussion in our next meeting.
- You will meet with your co-parent counselor to work on your time-share with the children as you transition into your nesting arrangement and separating households.
- *Agenda for next mediation*: child support, spousal support, and expenses.
- We are planning to meet again in mid to late June and we will circulate dates in a separate email.

Please let me know if you have any questions or clarifications to the above items. Thank you both.

Occasionally clients or counsel will suggest that no follow-up email is needed, often as a (misguided) cost-saving strategy. In those situations, the mediator should feel comfortable letting counsel and parties know the follow-up correspondence is part of the mediator's standard case handling procedures and ensures everyone—including the mediator—has a complete list of action items and next steps. In other words, this should not be an optional step, and the mediator should avoid asking if it would be helpful to send the email and instead just let everyone know that the next steps you've just reviewed together will be sent in a short follow-up email so everyone has the same information. If there is pushback from clients or counsel to attempt to minimize fees from the mediator, the mediator might respond by letting them know the mediator will need to finalize the list of action items in their own notes to track the status of action items either way (i.e., the time will be spent either way) and that this is an important part of the case management needed.

B. The Comprehensive Mediation Summary: A Recipe

The purpose of a more detailed Mediation Summary is to keep a current comprehensive summary of the case as a whole that can be updated after each full mediation session unless a shorter, bullet-point email is more appropriate, depending on the issues discussed or resolved.

A comprehensive Mediation Summary is a more time-consuming project than the quicker follow-up email, but it is an invaluable tool for the mediator and all involved in the case. If the clients pause the mediation for two months or two years, they can return to the last comprehensive Mediation Summary to know exactly where things were left on all issues, which would not be as easy with just the bullet-point follow-up correspondence. The Mediation

Summary can also be very helpful for attorneys who are not attending mediations to understand all issues in the case and to advise their clients on the tentative agreements and open issues.

In my practice, our Mediation Summaries include everything we know about the case with an eye on what will be needed once we start drafting the formal settlement agreement. We use this Mediation Summary format as a roadmap for what has already happened in the case and what still needs to happen for the parties to reach complete agreements on each of their issues and to complete each of the procedural steps in their specific case. There is very little if anything that is "boilerplate" or otherwise generalized for all clients in the Mediation Summary, since each bullet point relates to the specific issues and discussion points of each particular case.

While mediator practices vary, the following is our recipe for the perfect Mediation Summary, which we have developed over many years, and like the rest of our practice, we are always adjusting as our work continues to evolve to best serve our clients. We prepare this after the first full mediation, update it when there are substantive updates to provide after each subsequent mediation, and share the updates with the parties and professionals:

- **Statistical Details.** Parents' and children's legal names, birth dates, date of marriage, any issues about date of separation, restoration of former names, changes to children's names, current addresses, and any other relevant statistical details. This is the information that will be in the case initiation documents with the court and will also be included in the formal settlement agreement once that stage is reached.
- **Court Case Details.** Status of the petition, response, service issues, status conferences, court hearings, existing orders, and other signed agreements (i.e., temporary stipulations or premarital and postmarital agreements).
- **Professionals Involved.** Identification of any family law counsel (and whether they are representing or consulting), estate counsel, accountants, financial advisors, and any other professionals. We also include the dates of each mediation here and note any prior mediators or prior attorneys in this section, so that everything we know about the case and the individuals involved is included in one place.
- **Next Steps/Action Items.** Next steps for everyone—parties, counsel, mediator, forensic accountant, co-parent counselor, and other professionals—should be itemized and kept up to date in this section, including the agenda for the next mediation so everyone can be prepared.

- Examples of action items in this section might be one or both parties discussing tax filing options with their tax professional for the current or next tax year, obtaining the equity vesting documents for a time rule analysis, discussing specific issues with their family or estate attorneys, deciding whether to have the mediator or estate counsel draft real property transfer documents to be signed once the formal agreements are signed, providing specific documents needed for the financial disclosures, or working offline together on the division of household furnishings or collections.
- Examples of action items for the professionals might be that the mediator will send updated support calculations or follow up with the parties' estate counsel to discuss specific issues and report back to the group; or it could be one party's family law counsel working on preparing corporate transfer documents with their client's corporate counsel and sharing by a certain date, or the co-parent counselor working to finalize the parenting plan with the clients.
- These are just a few of the action items the mediator might include under a single heading so the clients don't need to sift through all the emails and/or complete Mediation Summary to create their own follow-up list. The mediator can also copy/paste just this section of the Mediation Summary into an email to help keep everyone on track if the full Mediation Summary feels too overwhelming (this is case- and client-dependent, of course).

- **Overall Goals or Global Approach.** Depending on the circumstances and personalities in the case, the mediator might find it helpful to include an overview of the parties' goals and/or overall approach to their asset division. This can be particularly useful when the overall approach deviates from established legal principles. Consider this a lead-in to the itemized substantive issues in the next sections. This section might help explain why certain assets are being divided in the manner agreed to, as a reminder for clients or an explanation to separate consulting counsel, financial advisors, or parenting professionals. This section can highlight shared or separate goals the separate attorneys or other professionals might not be aware of in the absence of this note in the Mediation Summary. Here are a few examples of what might be useful in this section:
  - "Your overall shared goals include Asher remaining in the Family Home for at least the next four years and ensuring Winnie can plan for early retirement at age 63."

- In a case with substantial separate inherited property that the parties have carefully considered and decided together to treat in a manner different than how the court might treat it, and which affects multiple asset categories in the case, it can be helpful to note the reasons or just their high-level approach, such as: "You both recognize the court would not divide your separate property assets between you and you both feel comfortable considering all assets to be shared based on your financial history and decisions you have made as a family."
- Or, in a long-term marriage with no premarriage or other separate assets, it could be helpful to include in this section something broad like: "You both agree there are no premarriage assets or other separate property assets for either of you and that all assets were created during marriage."
- Or the mediator can identify an alternative structure created by the parties, such as: "You have agreed to use Jane's February 1, 2024, date of separation for all purposes except for Ariel's retirement account, which you agree to divide based on Ariel's date of separation of June 30, 2025. This is based on our detailed factual and legal discussion on these issues and what you each feel is most important to you and trying to reach compromises you both feel good about."

- **Substantive Settlement Issues or Tentative Agreements.** Whatever title you select, think of this section as the meat of the Mediation Summary recipe and of the clients' agreements. This is where the mediator outlines the details of all substantive issues, which may include child support, spousal support, asset and debt division (including separate headings for each asset and debt classification and any equalizing payment or reimbursement issues), tax filing issues, health and life insurance, pets, and any other substantive issues in the case. Tentative agreements on each of the substantive issues should be outlined in summary format and not formal legal language, since this is not a formal agreement and any open questions can be flagged in each subsection so parties and any counsel are aware of the specific questions that still need to be resolved before formal agreements can be reached and language perfected.

Here is an example of how this section of the Mediation Summary might look in a very straightforward case. You will see that even in an uncomplicated case, there are a great number of details to organize to make sure everyone is aligned with these terms before this all gets drafted into a formal settlement agreement. For ease of reference, we include heading numbers, which we have picked up at Section III in this example:

III. Income, Expenses, and Spousal Support

- You have already separated out your paychecks and automatic withdrawals and are each paying for your own expenses and 50 percent of the home expenses pending sale.
- Your current base salaries are roughly equivalent with fluctuating bonus compensation.
- We discussed options for spousal support (aka alimony), including monthly modifiable or nonmodifiable spousal support, a lump-sum buyout, a zero support order subject to modifiability if there is a change in circumstances later, or a mutual waiver of spousal support regardless of any changes in the future for either of you. You agree there will be a complete mutual waiver of any spousal support rights in this "short-term" marriage (i.e., fewer than ten years) regardless of any circumstances or changes of income for either of you in the future.

IV. Health and Life Insurance

- **Health Insurance.** You are both currently covered under Mary's group health coverage through her employment with ABC Corporation. Mary agrees to maintain spousal coverage for Ben through the end of February 2026, when your marital status will be terminated. Ben's prepayment of his share of premiums to Mary through February 2026 has been factored into your expense reconciliation reimbursement. Upon entry of final judgment in March 2026, Mary will notify her benefits administrator of the marital status termination and Ben will have the right to elect up to 36 months of continuing coverage under COBRA (at Ben's expense).
- **Life Insurance.** You each have term life policies through your employers and no cash value policies. You agree you will each be assigned your own policies with no requirements to maintain minimum coverage for the other spouse.

V. Assets and Debts

1234 A Street, Townie, CA 98765 Family Home

- Purchased during marriage in May 2020; held in both names individually, with a joint Bank of America mortgage (loan *3434) with $250,355 balance as of June 30, 2025.
- You agree to sell the home as soon as possible and have jointly signed a listing agreement.

- You agree to share equally in the home sale proceeds subject to the agreed reimbursement to Mary of $100,000, which will be included in your escrow instructions to the title company (i.e., $100,000 is owed from Ben's 50 percent share of the proceeds and not from the community equity before division of the proceeds between you).
- You will share equally in all costs of sale including the anticipated capital gain tax liability after your combined $500,000 exclusion from capital gain this year. If the home does not sell this year, you will each report your 50 percent of the gain in your separate returns for next year and will each claim your separate $250,000 exclusion from capital gain and will each pay the resulting tax liability for your 50 percent of the remaining taxable gain.

Household Furnishings/Items/Jewelry/Artwork/Collections

- You worked together outside of mediation to divide your household furnishings, collections, and personal items, with no remaining issues or equalizing needed. We will include in your formal agreements that you are each assigned the furnishings and other household and personal items and collections in each of your own possessions.

Vehicles

- Ben is assigned the 2024 Audi Q5 (no debt) and all associated expenses; assigned without offset in your overall asset division.
- Mary is assigned the 2021 Ford F-250 truck and auto loan in her sole name and all associated expenses; assigned without offset in your overall asset division.

Bank and Investment Accounts

- There are no joint bank accounts to divide/close.
- You will each be assigned the bank and investment accounts in your own names without equalization/offset:
  - Mary is assigned the Chase Bank checking (account *1212) and savings (account *1313).
  - Ben is assigned the Bank of America checking (account *2828) and savings (account *3939).

Retirement Plans

- You will each be assigned the retirement accounts in your own names [and list the accounts here]. Ben will waive the $32,000 pretax equalization of the $64,000 difference in your respective retirement assets in exchange for Mary waiving $25,000 in posttax reimbursements owed by Ben to Mary, reducing the total reimbursements from $125,000 to $100,000, which has been accounted for in the division of home sale proceeds above.

- Ben will be solely responsible for the tax liability associated with his 2025 IRA distribution.

Employer Equity

- Company A common stock in Ben's name (250,000 shares fully vested); you agree this is assigned to Ben.
- Company B 65,000 vested and 125,000 unvested shares of stock in Mary's name; you agree this is assigned to Mary.
- You agree the estimated value of employer equity (including your compromise value of the unvested equity) is roughly equivalent and you each agree to waive equalization for any difference in the current or future values.

Other Assets

- **Life Insurance.** There are no cash value policies to allocate (other than term group life insurance through your respective employer group policies noted earlier).
- **Paid Time Off.** You agree you are each assigned your own without offset.
- **Miles/Reward Points.** You agree you are each assigned your own without offset.
- **Club Memberships/Season Tickets.** There are no such assets to discuss/allocate.

Debts/Credit Cards

- You agree you will each be assigned the credit cards and loans in your own names.
- Ben's American Express personal loan is assigned to Ben and has been factored into your overall asset division/offsets.
- There are no credit cards or other loans/debts in joint names.

Equalizing Payment

- Based on your overall settlement structure and reconciliation of expenses via the home sale distributions, neither of you will make a payment to the other to equalize the division of your assets and debts and there are no remaining reimbursements owed after this asset division.

VI. Professional Fees

- **Mediation Fees.** *TBD if you will share equally in the neutral mediation fees or a different allocation.
- **Attorney's Fees.** *TBD if you will share equally, each pay for your own separate consulting attorneys, or a different allocation.

VII. Other Issues

- **Estate Planning.** There are no estate planning issues to include in your Marital Settlement Agreement (i.e., no joint trust to dissolve, wills to update, powers of attorney, etc.).
- **Waivers.** Your agreement will include a waiver of all claims including financial issues, civil/tort claims, of any kind whatsoever, unless you let us know otherwise or would like to discuss this.
- **Pets.** You agree to share equally in the costs and responsibilities for your two family dogs, Minnie and Winnie, and will continue to share equal time via your alternating week on/week off timeshare schedule.

VIII. Taxes

- **Tax Year 2024.** You agree to file jointly in April 2025 with allocation of liability/refunds to be allocated based on your own income/assets for the full tax year based on your December 28, 2023, date of separation; you will work with your accountant to determine your respective total tax liability.
- **Tax Year 2025.** You agree to terminate your marital status as of February 28, 2026; if there is an advantage to one of you to file jointly for tax year 2025, you will file jointly and allocate liability/refunds based on your own income/assets, sharing equally in the liability and deductions associated with the family home, and allocating the IRA distributions to Ben. If there is a disadvantage to the other person, the advantaged spouse will make up the difference to eliminate the disadvantage. You will work together and with your tax professionals.

You will see from the preceding sample "Substantive Settlement Issues or Tentative Agreements" section of the Mediation Summary that this is not intended to be a formal settlement agreement. All agreements are tentative until they are memorialized into a formal agreement and signed by both parties. The Mediation Summary is just a summary or informal term sheet and should not be mistaken as or treated as an enforceable agreement. The mediator may need to remind the parties in a mediation session: "This is the Mediation Summary, where we just list out in bullet-point format the terms being considered on each issue. Once you have both confirmed these terms, we can begin drafting your formal Marital Settlement Agreement."

This means the Mediation Summary does not and should not include formal legal language with all the detailed protections for both parties, such as indemnifications, hold harmless language, or other complex terminology not used in the mediation discussions. Instead, it is a summary outline of the terms agreed to by the parties in mediation—not necessarily "high level," since we include all the agreements that have been reached and are being considered, but it should look and feel different from a formal legal agreement.

As additional tentative agreements are reached or procedural milestones completed, the comprehensive Mediation Summary can be updated so there is a current up-to-date summary of the current status of all issues. Our practice is to share tracked or redlined versions as well as clean versions for each successive iteration, though we may start a draft tracked update and keep it as a draft in our file until additional updates warrant sharing a more comprehensively updated Mediation Summary. We find it useful for clients and counsel to be able to reference the evolution of edits, agreements, and additional details in each successive version of the Mediation Summary.

Our goal is to use the Mediation Summary along with the formal financial disclosures to draft the formal Marital Settlement Agreement once all open issues have been resolved. Will there be additional details and questions that come up in the drafting of the formal agreements even after the open TBDs are resolved? Possibly. But this format ensures everyone knows what they are agreeing to before it gets drafted into a formal legal contract. And each party can take the Mediation Summary to their own separate attorneys or consultants to walk through every issue and open question in preparation for the next mediation or in preparation for giving approval to the mediator to move ahead with drafting the formal agreements.

C. Next Steps at Every Step

In addition to follow-up emails or Mediation Summaries after each meeting, every email to the parties and/or counsel should include next steps since it is the mediator's role to keep everyone on track. And while counsel and other family law professionals likely have their own case management notes and reminders, they do not have the same role as the neutral mediator who is shepherding the case and all the individuals through the case process and monitoring everyone's action items and next steps. For example, if a client, counsel, or mediator emails about four issues and there is a response to just one issue, the mediator can respond on the thread with: "Thank you for your follow-up on this issue. We will look forward to hearing back regarding items two through four before our meeting next Tuesday."

I like to think of every action item in a case being a tennis ball and the ball either needs to be in the mediator's "court" (i.e., there is a specific action item for my office or me) or someone else's court (i.e., there is a specific action item for one or more individuals) and everyone on the team (i.e., parties, counsel, mediator, etc.) needs to know whose court the ball is in so nothing slips between the cracks and gets missed or forgotten. In our practice, each of our emails to clients and counsel lets everyone know what is happening, where the "ball" is, and where it needs to go next. And we set follow-up reminders at various intervals to make sure everyone remains on track. While the mediator's job is not to unduly badger or micromanage clients or counsel, or aggressively police each step of the case, family law cases benefit from the anchoring that neutral case management provides. Once it is clear the mediator is in control of the case details and everyone's action items, the clients and counsel know they can rely on the neutral mediator's case management skills to shepherd everyone toward the finish line and give a helping hand to anyone who needs it to get back and stay on track.

One of my goals in every case is to check in on the status or give a status update before anyone else comes around looking for an update. For example, in cases in which we are waiting for the forensic accountant to complete a project, if I'm wondering why I haven't heard from the accountant, others in the case may be wondering the same thing. It is more efficient and reflects the mediator's case management role and control of the process for the mediator to check in with the neutral accountant to align on timing; this ensures the mediator can give neutral updates to the group rather than one side asking the accountant for an update that might not be shared with the mediator or the other side.

Staying ahead of everyone is not always possible; however, anticipating concerns about timing or other next steps is something the mediator can strive to do so everyone knows what to expect up front and everyone has the same updates from the neutral case managing mediator. In addition, including next steps in every email is a helpful way of managing and corralling all the loose ends. If a client emails about one issue, we can respond to the request and at the end of the email, let them know what to expect next.

Ending each email by identifying next steps is helpful not only for the clients and counsel who receive these reminders about what happens next, but it is also helpful for the mediator (and their staff) to know what was said to the clients about next steps in case there are any adjustments that are needed when something else happens in the case. For example, if we are waiting for something to happen before we schedule our next meeting, but there is a change in the expected timing for one of those steps, we can email our clients to let them know and suggest an adjustment, such as: "We previously discussed waiting to hear about the details of Bill's severance before we schedule our next mediation. But since it sounds like that may not be available for another three to four weeks and given that there are other time-sensitive issues you both want to discuss, it might make sense to schedule a shorter meeting now to discuss those time-sensitive issues and then wait until the severance details are clear in a few more weeks before we meet again to discuss support and expenses."

To maintain a productive working relationship with all team members, the mediator should be mindful of setting and managing the tone of the emails to minimize any hostility or overly adversarial language that might creep in from parties or counsel. As the team leader, the mediator can model respectful and solution-oriented communication, fostering collegiality and collaboration among the team of clients and professionals.

For example, in an email discussion in which counsel have agreed to an issue, such a response might be "Sure that works" or "Yes, that would be agreeable to Nancy." What's next though? The mediator needs to respond to clarify or confirm the next steps and timing, such as: "Great—I am glad that solution is workable for both of you and your clients. It sounds like we are ready to draft the stipulation on temporary support, which I will plan to get out to you both by end of day tomorrow so you can each review the draft with your clients. We are scheduled for a case management meeting next Friday and we can discuss any proposed edits together at that time. Please let me know if you have any questions. Thank you." Let's break that email down a little to analyze the reasons for each piece:

- ***Great—I am glad that solution is workable for both of you and your clients.*** This acknowledges their collaborative efforts and reflects the mediator's understanding that both counsel have agreed to a specific issue. While "that solution" may be appropriate when the email discussion makes it clear exactly what was agreed to, other situations may require a more detailed recitation of what was agreed to, such as: "Thank you both for confirming you are both agreeable to the compromise temporary monthly spousal support of $5,000 starting November 1, 2025."
- ***It sounds like we are ready to draft the stipulation on temporary support[.]*** This notifies both counsel of the next step and allows an

opportunity for either counsel to chime in if they think we are not ready for this step yet.

- ***[W]hich I will plan to get out to you both by end of day tomorrow[.]*** This confirms a previously discussed plan as to which professional will take the lead on drafting the formal agreement and the estimated timeframe so everyone knows what to expect and when.
- ***[S]o you can each review the draft with your clients.*** This notifies both counsel what the next step will be once they receive the mediator's draft stipulation.
- ***We are scheduled for a case management meeting next Friday and we can discuss any proposed edits together at that time.*** This reminds both counsel of the next meeting already scheduled and the plan for sharing proposed edits. If there is no meeting scheduled, the mediator can suggest meeting times for discussing any proposed edits to the draft stipulation together.
- ***Please let me know if you have any questions.*** This gives an opening for questions about next steps. If there are more substantive details included in the email, the mediator may instead say: "Please let me know if there are any questions or clarifications either of you feel may be needed regarding the summary above."
- ***Thank you.*** The mediator should always lead and finish with professional and polite communication; this can also read "Thank you both" or, if the situation calls for it, "Thank you both for all your hard work on this." Because this is a difficult process, it can be helpful to applaud clients and counsel for reaching agreements and pursuing a collaborative path.

Keeping everyone on track means keeping track of action items, modifying action items, and reminding clients and counsel (with patience and without judgment) about agreed steps. Including each action item in follow-up emails helps to avoid variations of: "Oh I didn't realize you needed that" or: "I didn't know you were waiting on me for that." Or even: "We didn't talk about that." This is why next steps at every step should be made clear—so everyone is operating with the same to-do list, there are reminders of what is still needed, and there is acknowledgment when steps are completed and what the next steps are now.

Keeping everyone on track also means responding in a timely manner to group emails (the same or next day) with clients or counsel to ensure the discussion continues to be managed and shepherded to the next stage by the neutral mediator.

10

Formalizing Agreements: The Marital Settlement Agreement

A. The Advantages of Neutral Drafting

Once all the issues that need to be resolved have been discussed and agreed upon, it is time to draft the formal settlement agreement. These are known in various jurisdictions as the marital settlement agreement, divorce settlement agreement, separation agreement, or matrimonial agreement. There are also confidential marital settlement agreements and stipulated judgments, depending on the jurisdiction. Regardless of the form of the final agreements and even when our mediation office is not involved in a particular case, I always recommend that the mediator prepare the first draft of the formal settlement agreement from their neutral perspective. As the central information hub and team leader who has been managing all the details and personalities in the case, there is nobody better positioned to prepare the first draft of the formal agreements.

When separate attorneys prepare the first drafts of settlement agreements, assumptions can easily be made that favor one party or the other, whether due to implicit or overt bias on the part of the separate attorney. This is not to say that most separate attorneys have ill intentions or would consciously trample over the other party's legal rights (or feelings) when drafting legal provisions favorable to their own client, but there is no question that the responsibility of the separate attorney is to protect the interests of their own client, whereas the neutral mediator's responsibility is to both parties. The mediator has worked with both parties, is acutely aware of their respective concerns and sensitivities, and has a heightened focus on balancing both parties' rights, interests, and needs. When it comes to drafting legal provisions from the perspective of protecting both parties' interests (legally and emotionally), there is clear logic in tasking the neutral mediator with this responsibility.

Although the case managing mediator will be preparing detailed mediation summaries for the clients' (and attorneys') approval prior to drafting formal agreements (as detailed in Chapter 9), questions inevitably arise in drafting the detailed language of the formal agreements. In drafting formal agreements, the mediator should identify any questions or details that may not have been fully fleshed out in the mediation discussions or that may need further discussion rather than making assumptions that have not been agreed upon. The parties are looking to the mediator to reflect only the agreements that have been explicitly made, to identify the issues that still need discussing, and possibly to provide options for both parties to consider even at this late stage of the case.

While mediators are still human and missteps can happen, our years of neutral mediation experience hone our internal antennae to focus on both parties' interests. As a result, we are attuned to drafting issues that might result in an advantage or disadvantage to one party over the other or result in one party feeling something is unbalanced (even if legally that is not the case), or which rely on assumptions or details not specifically agreed to and that need to be flagged. The mediator has worked with both parties and their counsel throughout the case and can work on drafting balanced language in the first draft. The mediator can also provide multiple options for consideration in the draft agreement or just highlight an issue for further discussion when numerous options exist that have not yet been discussed.

Here are a few examples of how these issues can arise and what the mediator can include in the formal draft settlement agreement or in a follow-up email to clients and/or counsel:

Case Example 1. Bill and Beth have agreed that Bill will maintain health insurance coverage for Beth and their children through the end of the calendar year when the parties' marital status will be terminated. Bill's attorney might assume Beth will be reimbursing Bill for Beth's share of the health insurance premiums for her and the children and would include that assumption in drafting the formal agreement, whereas the mediator should recognize that this detail was not specifically discussed or agreed on and can include a question or highlight in the formal agreement. The notation might say: "*TBD whether this is with or without reimbursement from Beth and for what portion/amount" in order to flag this issue for further discussion.

Case Example 2. Joan and Salma have agreed to co-own real property for an agreed-upon period and have worked through the details of their co-ownership. If Salma's attorney prepares the first draft of the formal agreement, the attorney might check to get Salma's preference on estate planning provisions in the event of either party's death during the co-ownership and may not see this as disadvantageous to the other party. If the mediator drafts the formal agreement, the mediator would recognize that the parties' discussions did not include estate planning options during the co-ownership period and would include options in the draft settlement agreement for the parties to consider based on the context of their co-ownership agreements. The mediator might include the following note to the parties: "*TBD estate planning issues/rights upon death during co-ownership; options may include the deceased spouse's interests being inherited by the children or the other spouse, or each party having discretion to gift your 50 percent ownership interests pursuant to your own separate trusts or estate plans; or you may want to discuss options with your trust and estate counsel."

Case Example 3. Patrick and Hunter have struggled with power imbalances throughout their relationship and in the mediation. When drafting the formal agreement based on the terms agreed to in mediation, the mediator will be on the lookout to catch drafting language that might result in Hunter feeling that they are not being treated equally in all respects as Patrick, even if the issue or language does not actually afford any legal benefits to Hunter. Even something the separate attorneys may perceive as innocuous could be problematic, such as: "Patrick shall have 30 calendar days from the effective date of this agreement to remove Hunter from the Chase Visa (account *9898)," but in a different section of the agreement: "Hunter shall have 60 calendar days from the effective date of this agreement to provide Patrick with an electronic copy of the parties' digital photo library." While these issues appear quite distinct, unless both timeframes were discussed and specifically agreed to in mediation, the mediator would want to ensure in the first draft of the agreement, particularly in this case, that both parties receive equal time for handling any postsigning actions even if there could be an argument for one action needing more time than the other.

Case Example 4. Amy and Victor have reached time-share agreements regarding their minor children, including some holiday scheduling. A separate attorney drafting the formal agreements might "assign" certain holidays between the parents without a mutual discussion. This could be the result of one party, Amy, asking her attorney to assume her preferred holiday schedule will be agreed upon while Victor is put on the defensive because terms not agreed upon have been included in the agreement. The mediator knows they have two clients to answer to and would not include one party's preference without a discussion and would instead highlight that this issue of holidays needs to be discussed.

In other words, no matter how perceptive or sensitive the separate attorneys in a case may be, their role throughout the case is distinct from the mediator's role of managing the sensitivities of both clients in a meaningful way to lead them to the stage of being able to draft a formal agreement from a neutral perspective. It is far easier for a separate attorney to unintentionally bump up against the other party's sensitivities in drafting the formal agreement, which can ultimately have a devastating impact on how or whether the case reaches the stage of a signed agreement.

B. MOUs and Other Enforceable Term Sheets

Many attorneys or mediators prefer to use enforceable term sheets, referred to variously as a Memorandum of Understanding (MOU) or Memorandum of Agreements (MOA). In California, attorneys often refer to these as "CCP 664.6 stipulations," which is a reference to the statutory provision of California Civil Code section 664.6, which allows the court to enforce agreements that have been stipulated to in a signed writing by the parties or in court.

While there are variations in mediator and attorney practices as well as local and state requirements about which professionals can draft certain types of agreements, and the needs of each case certainly vary as well, our preferred practice is not to prepare an enforceable term sheet in mediation as this gives the feeling of a time-pressured settlement process instead of the thoughtful process we strive to create for our clients. Our preference is to follow the path of reaching agreements together over the course of multiple sessions with time for reflection between meetings until all remaining TBDs in the Mediation Summary have been resolved, with both clients approving the terms outlined in the Mediation Summary before we draft the formal agreement for everyone's review and approval. This mediation-focused path tends to feel much more collaborative than the more litigation-focused alternative of ensuring the parties sign an enforceable term sheet before they leave the mediation session. However, there are some cases in which the need for an enforceable term sheet is clear. In addition, some family law professionals prefer an enforceable term sheet immediately following the mediation and not necessarily in the mediation itself. The pros and cons of signed term sheets vary from case to case but are generally the following:

Pros

- A signed agreement of any kind clearly signals commitment to the terms.
- There is a lower likelihood that either party will back out of agreements reached if they have each signed.
- Time-sensitive actions might be able to be initiated with a signed term sheet.

Cons

- There is typically time pressure to finalize the details of term sheets, whether prepared during a mediation session or immediately afterward. Drafting under pressure can lead to missed details or terms and the inability to draft more protective and clear language, which would be included in a more detailed Marital Settlement Agreement (which requires more time and effort than a term sheet).
- Vague terms in a signed term sheet can easily lead to enforceability challenges in court.
- Reserved issues that cannot be resolved before the term sheet is signed can lead to difficulty later resolving a reserved standalone issue when all other issues have been included in the signed term sheet and can result in litigation.
- For cost-sensitive clients, the additional professional fees and time to draft two agreements (the term sheet and the full Marital Settlement Agreement) leads many clients to request skipping a signed term sheet and devoting the available resources to drafting a single comprehensive settlement agreement.

C. Managing the Editing Stage

The mediator should expect and welcome edits to formal agreements from clients and counsel. In my own mediation office, we don't send settlement agreements out without two sets of attorney–mediator eyes first reviewing and editing the agreement. This ensures one mediator's brain hasn't just filled in language that isn't there and provides the perspective of someone who doesn't necessarily know what the first mediator is trying to convey. In this way, we put ourselves in the shoes of a future judge or attorney needing to interpret the parties' agreements. This is part of our office's team-based approach, and I strongly believe our clients benefit from this approach in the quality of our work product. This is particularly true given that Marital Settlement Agreements can be 20 to 50 pages or more and not just short five- to ten-page stipulations.

Relying on the concept that two (or three) sets of eyes are better than one, the mediator can more easily remove their ego from the editing process and welcome ideas, clarifications, or edits from the clients who are at the heart of the case and from the other family law professionals in the case. These professionals may include the separate family law attorneys as well as parenting professionals and financial professionals, depending on their level of involvement. This team approach improves collegiality and benefits the clients in the quality and clarity of their final settlement agreement, ensuring the agreement not only reflects both parties' agreements and intentions on all issues, but is also clear to multiple readers from different perspectives. Remember, the separate attorneys are reading not only from their own clients' perspectives but also from the perspective of any challenges to enforceability in a hypothetical future court action, which means the mediator needs to think about enforceability in drafting formal language as well.

As the case manager, the mediator should keep track of all edits (i.e., "proposed edits") and ensure version control is maintained and followed, either with version numbers, dates, and names of each editor in the saved document title. Every office has their own protocols for saving and titling documents. Here is an example of how the first version and future subsequent iterations might be titled:

- First draft: "Jones & Smith Marital Settlement Agreement v1-2025-03-30 (Mediator)."
- Followed by the second version from a separate attorney, which the mediator can retitle as: "Jones & Smith Marital Settlement Agreement v2-2025-04-05 (A. Brown tracked edits)."
- Followed by the third tracked and clean versions from the mediator after discussion with both counsel: "Jones & Smith Marital Settlement Agreement v3-2025-04-07 (Mediator tracked edits)" and "Jones & Smith Marital Settlement Agreement v3-2025-04-07 (Clean)." You can see that we label the redlined/tracked version with the author of the edits in the title but the clean version shared by the mediator is just labeled as "clean"—to be as clear as possible.

In addition to tracking versions and indicating whether a draft includes tracked edits or is a "clean" version, it can also be useful to have a secure document portal where clients and professionals in each case can access the initial drafts and each successive draft of the formal agreements in the case in addition to other case documents. In our mediation office, this supports our goal of transparency, organization, and efficiency, all of which help to streamline the editing stage and get everyone to the final stage of signing the agreements.

Occasionally, separate attorneys directly exchange proposed edits to the formal settlement agreement outside of the mediation process. This is more common when the mediator has not had an ongoing case management role in the case and can also occur with preliminary stipulations when cases are just getting started. This is often the result of the separate attorneys not fully recognizing the case management role of the mediator and instead conducting their work in separate silos. This latter approach is more common with settlement-conference-style mediations, but can seep into cases even when there is a case managing mediator. In such cases, the mediator can simply ask to remain on the email threads to be able to keep track of the status and to know when to suggest check-in meetings to discuss issues as they arise.

The mediator can also follow up with clients or counsel at regular intervals to make sure everyone knows and remembers whose figurative "court" the agreement (i.e., the "ball") is in to manage everyone's expectations on timing and next steps. When clients are reviewing agreements on their own or with counsel consulting in the background, the mediator can check in after two or three weeks with an open-ended email, such as: "I am just checking in on your review of the formal settlement agreement to see if you have any questions or proposed edits or if you would like to schedule a follow-up meeting to work through the open issues together." If the separate attorneys are taking the lead, the mediator might adjust the check-in language to the attorneys to something more specific, such as: "I am writing to check in on your review of the formal settlement agreement with your clients and to set a timeline for exchanging proposed edits or schedule a follow-up meeting to discuss proposed edits together. Please let me know your preference for next steps."

If there are delays in getting proposed edits back from counsel via email, the mediator can recommend deadlines and get agreements to keep things moving forward. Alternatively, the mediator can recommend a mediation session with clients or case management meeting with counsel to discuss proposed edits, brainstorm options for resolving competing interests, identify any remaining open issues, and agree on timing for next steps. Next steps can include scheduling a follow-up meeting or dates for the parties or counsel to respond to proposed edits.

Because mediation cases often do not have hard deadlines in the way that litigated cases do, it can be helpful for the mediator to set deadlines for counsel to include in their calendars so their follow-up work remains a priority. For example, the mediator can include the following suggestions in an email to counsel: "I would like to suggest that we schedule a follow-up meeting the week of April 21st and with both counsel exchanging proposed edits the week prior to that on April 14th. I have included my availability for our meeting below and look forward to hearing from you with your availability and confirmation of this plan."

When it comes to setting deadlines for clients without representing attorneys, the mediator should take their cues from the parties themselves. Some clients take months to focus on and review their formal agreements with their consulting attorneys. If both clients are working at the same pace, the mediator does not need to push things forward but can still check in. The mediator might include something like the following in a check-in email to clients: "There is no rush from our side, and we will look forward to hearing from you whenever you are both ready to discuss any proposed edits to your agreement. If we haven't heard from you in the next four to six weeks, we will check in with you to find out if you are still planning to finalize your case this year or if you plan to keep things on hold until the new year." However, when one party is eager and ready to sign the agreement and the other party is operating at a much slower pace, the mediator can request a separate meeting with the "less ready" client and/or with their attorney to help move the review and finalization process forward.

As with all communications by the mediator, the mediator should always strike a balance between being professional while providing the respectful but helpful nudging needed by the clients and counsel and any other professionals who may be involved at this stage of the case. An example check-in email might be the following:

> I am writing to check in on the timing for both counsel's edits to the January 5th draft Marital Settlement Agreement. Since we are heading into February, it would be helpful if we can set a timeline for next steps so everyone knows what to expect.
>
> Please let me know if both counsel will be able to share proposed edits by Friday, February 7, by email or whether you prefer to schedule a meeting the first or second week of February to discuss and work through any proposed edits together. Thank you.

With subsequent versions of the settlement agreement, the mediator should always identify what is being shared. In cases with counsel taking the lead and clients in the background, the mediator might send the following email to counsel:

> Thank you both for sharing your proposed edits to the first draft of the Marital Settlement Agreement. Based on your follow-up emails approving both sets of edits, I have incorporated both sets of edits into the attached [or

uploaded] Marital Settlement Agreement v2 (including the tracked version and the clean version).

Please let us know if you have any additional proposed edits or if you and your clients are both comfortable with this version 2 as the final version of the Marital Settlement Agreement. If there are no further proposed edits, we will circulate the clean version 2 for everyone's electronic signatures via AdobeSign.

Either way, we will look forward to hearing from you both. Thank you.

In cases without attorneys, the mediator might send the following email:

We have received Allie's proposed edits to the first draft of the Marital Settlement Agreement and will look forward to hearing from Ayman to let us know if there are any additional proposed edits. Alternatively, we can schedule a follow-up meeting to discuss and work through any open questions or issues together.

Either way, we look forward to hearing from you regarding these next steps. Thank you.

In the event that Ayman in the preceding example responds that there are no additional edits at this time and that Allie's edits are agreed to by Ayman, the mediator would then email the revised agreement and next steps so both clients know what to expect, as set forth in the following sample email:

Thank you, Ayman, for confirming you are in agreement with Allie's proposed edits and have no further edits at this time. We have incorporated the agreed-upon edits into the attached [or uploaded] Marital Settlement Agreement v2 (including the tracked version and the clean version).

Please let us know if you are both comfortable with this version 2 as the final version of your Marital Settlement Agreement. Once we hear from both of you confirming you are ready to sign, we will circulate the clean version 2 for your electronic signatures via AdobeSign [or DocuSign] along with the judgment documents required by the court to finalize your divorce.

Once we have your signatures on all documents, we will prepare the judgment packet for submission to the court and will update you on any timing issues or next steps.

Please let us know if you have any questions regarding these next steps. Otherwise, we look forward to hearing from each of you to confirm you are ready to sign your Marital Settlement Agreement. Thank you.

In all correspondence, the mediator can strive to check in and guide without pushing, and to let everyone know the current status and what to expect next. In this way, the mediator ensures clients and professionals know the mediator is still guiding the case and will continue to do so all the way to the final steps of signing the agreements and waiting for the court to approve the final judgment.

11

Final Steps for Obtaining the Final Judgment

The neutral case managing mediator takes responsibility for shepherding the case all the way through the final stages of the court case, which benefits clients and separate counsel by having a neutral professional keeping an objective eye on every step of the process through completion. This means that once the parties and any other professionals have reviewed, edited, and approved the formal Marital Settlement Agreement, the mediator should coordinate the signing of the agreements and judgment documents by clients and counsel before preparing and submitting the judgment packet and then circulating the final approved judgment to the group upon receipt from the court.

A. Judgment Documents

In our mediation practice, we prepare the judgment documents and request input and approval from any counsel involved. We take on this role because we plan to submit the judgment packet directly to the court. Preparing and being in control of the judgment documents allows us to be immediately responsive to the court if any requests or processing issues arise, whereas if a separate attorney prepares and submits the judgment documents, the mediator has less visibility into submission dates, court delays, or other processing issues that can surface.

As noted earlier, in counties that do not yet permit attorney–mediators to file documents on behalf of both parties, or in cases involving a non-attorney mediator, the formal agreements and judgment documents may need to be prepared with one party or one counsel's information in the case caption. This workaround should not stop the neutral mediator from taking responsibility for managing the steps related to obtaining the final judgment to the fullest extent possible for the benefit of both clients.

There are some mediations in which the clients agree that one party's attorney will be responsible for preparing the judgment documents and submission to the court; this is often a suggestion made in the interest of shifting responsibility for professional fees. Although we typically suggest having the neutral mediator take on these responsibilities due to the follow-up that may be requested by the court or the responsibility for circulating updates and final approved judgments and any related orders to all team members, this is not always the best course for a case and can be discussed before embarking on these steps. Even in cases in which another office submits the judgment filing, the mediator should continue in their role of case manager, checking with the court for updates on the judgment processing and reporting back to the group so everyone has the same information from the perspective of the neutral mediator.

This is not (and should never be) a matter of keeping control for reasons of professional ego or retaining billable work by the mediator, but is instead part of the neutral case management that we encourage from start to finish of each case for everyone's benefit. If both counsel and parties agree with the plan for one party's attorney to prepare and submit the judgment filings, the mediator can support the clients and team and does not need to reject (or resent) the idea and can ensure the team knows the extent to which the mediator will manage any follow-up.

B. Coordinating Signings

There are several options for obtaining everyone's signatures on the agreements and judgment documents. If there is a court requirement for one signature to be notarized, our practice is to have both parties' signatures notarized unless there is a logistical hurdle such as the other party living abroad, in which case the time and cost for such a notarization may outweigh the desire for equivalent treatment when it is not a legal requirement.

Ideally, both parties could meet at the mediator's office to sign and notarize everything at once. If representing counsel are involved, the attorneys can email or mail their signatures in or drop them off in person or attend the signing with clients. I have also had the experience in which each client signs at their own attorney's office and the attorneys coordinate via courier between themselves and ultimately drop the original signed agreements and judgment documents to the mediator's office to prepare the judgment submission.

In California, when both parties have appeared in the case, there is no requirement that signatures to a Marital Settlement Agreement be notarized, in which case California's law permitting electronic signatures allows us to obtain electronic signatures via certificate applications such as AdobeSign and DocuSign. When electronic signatures are permitted, this greatly simplifies the signing step since the mediator's office can circulate the agreements and judgment documents to clients and counsel for automatic collection of electronic signatures, receive notifications when each document has been viewed and signed, and share fully executed copies automatically with all signatories.

Once everyone has signed the formal agreements and judgment documents, the mediator should ensure that everyone involved is updated. For example, if there is a parenting professional involved with the parties but who has not been on all mediation email discussions, they should be informed and provided a copy of the signed agreement. If there is a neutral forensic accountant or other financial professional, they should also be informed that the agreements have been signed and be provided with the signed agreement, if appropriate. This allows the other professionals on the case to know their work may be complete and, unless there are ongoing issues, that they can close their files. Whether they have ongoing work in the matter or not, the mediator shows their respect for the role and importance of the other neutral professionals in working as a team to help the clients get to this stage; these professionals deserve the professional satisfaction of knowing their work resulted in a final signed agreement along with all the other professionals.

C. Judgment Submission

Once the formal agreements and judgment documents have been signed by clients and any representing counsel, the mediator's office can prepare the complete judgment packet for submission. In our practice, our legal assistant team prepares the required copies, envelopes, and correspondence to the court and one of our attorney–mediators comprehensively reviews each document—at least as thoroughly as any family court examiner would do—before each judgment packet is hand-delivered to the court whenever possible with discussion with the clerks regarding current processing times. When non-attorney mediators are managing these final stages, they may coordinate with a neutral attorney–mediator or other document preparation service, but they should not feel like they are no longer involved since their role is to manage the case from the outset to completion, regardless of who is tasked with individual pieces of the process. Of course, many counties now offer (or require) electronic rather than paper filings, which streamlines the submission step, with the exception of the issues noted earlier about mediators not being able to submit filings in certain counties.

At each step of the judgment processing, the mediator should update the parties and any professionals at the following milestones:

- Upon submission of the judgment packet to the court.
- Upon completion of any steps in the court's processing.
- Upon entry of judgment into the court's online register of actions/ court file.
- Upon receipt of the final approved judgment from the court.

As soon as the mediator submits the request for final judgment to the court, clients and counsel should be informed of the status and expected timing for the court to process the submission. Some counties take two to three weeks to process requests for final judgment, while other counties can take three to four months or more. For in-person filings, our couriers ask the clerks for current processing times so we can share this information with clients and counsel.

Here is a sample email to clients regarding their judgment submission to the court with a copy of their fully signed agreements and judgment forms (we capitalize the names of their specific documents in our emails):

> Hi Orla and Cian:
>
> Your judgment packet was submitted to the court today. We have uploaded the following documents to our Shared Dropbox Folder for your electronic files which are currently awaiting court processing:
>
> - Judgment Documents and Stipulated Judgment: These documents were filed with the court.
> - Confidential Marital Settlement Agreement: This Agreement was submitted to the court for judicial review only and will not become part of the public court record.
> - Correspondence: A copy of our correspondence that we submitted to the court with your complete judgment packet.
>
> Your Agreements are binding and enforceable as of your December 1, 2025, signing, which means you can now proceed with the two steps triggered by the "Effective Date" of your Agreement (i.e., the mortgage paydown and removing Cian's authorized user status on the Citibank credit card (account *1234)).
>
> We can expect the court to take three to four months to process and approve your final judgment of divorce. In the coming months, the court will complete the review of your judgment packet and, upon approval, will enter your final judgment into the court system and issue your final divorce date. We will share electronic copies of these documents upon receipt from the court

and will send an email update including an explanation of the documents and your case status at that time. Please let us know if you have any questions in the meantime. Thank you both.

The mediator should take any steps possible to monitor the status of the court's judgment processing. In most counties, this means checking the online Register of Actions or court log daily for any updates to pass along to parties and counsel or address directly with the court in the event something does not look quite right. For example, we see occasional court clerk errors (more in some courts than others) in which a rejection is issued based on the absence of a required document that was previously filed. Because we monitor our judgment filings daily, we can quickly follow up to let the court know we see their rejection note and are writing to provide a file-endorsed copy for their records showing that document was previously filed, so this does not slow down their review and processing.

We have also seen rejections on the incorrect basis that a certain document was not included in the judgment submission, and we can quickly let the court clerk know why the document is not required in this case. For instance, certain case types require specific judgment documents and occasionally we encounter a less-experienced clerk who gets it wrong. Because we attempt to stay on top of all submissions to the court, we are able to fix the problem before it leads to longer unnecessary delays in being sent back and resubmitted.

In our experience, checking online updates from the court helps to keep the court's judgment processing as smooth as possible. And, because someone in our office is monitoring the online court record daily following each judgment submission, we can share updates with clients and counsel the day the court record is updated, which helps to alleviate clients' anxiety, even though we may still have to wait to receive the filed approved judgment.

Here is an example of an interim update we might send to clients on the judgment status:

Hi Etsuko and Mikhail:

We have been checking with the court regarding the status of your judgment and the court has now approved your final judgment with a divorce date of December 31, 2026, as requested. [In some cases, we also attach the court's online record reflecting the entry of the final judgment when timing is of particular importance to the parties.]

As soon as we receive the filed copies of your final approved judgment and related documents from the court in the coming weeks, we will provide electronic copies of these documents to each of you. Thank you.

D. Final Approved Judgment

When we receive the final approved judgment from the court, we don't want to just send the judgment without considering what else clients might need to know. We always include their official date of divorce, any explanations we think might be helpful, and any additional information or follow-up steps that may still be needed to complete the court case and to close the mediation file.

Here is an example of what not to send to clients: "Hi Molly and Jess: Please see your attached final judgment. Thank you." This leaves unanswered questions that can be easily answered with a little anticipation of what clients might be thinking when they receive such an email. The clients don't know if this is the last communication they will receive from the mediator or whether there are follow-up steps and who will be handling those. My guidance is to never leave clients wondering, "Ok, so now what?"

Here is a sample email we might send to clients with their final approved judgment, in which a Confidential Marital Settlement Agreement has been reviewed by a private judge and not submitted to the court (though there are other mechanisms for submitting confidential agreements to the court without engaging a private judge), and regarding the remaining steps in their case:

> Hi Sam and Tomas:
>
> We have now received your final approved judgment from the court and have attached the following documents to this email.
>
> - Final Approved Judgment (FL-180 with attached Stipulated Judgment).
> - One-page Filed Notice of Entry of Judgment (FL-190).
> - Confidential Marital Settlement Agreement: Reviewed and approved by your Private Judge and which is not a part of the public court file.
>
> You will see in the box located on the front of the Judgment and Notice of Entry of Judgment that your marital status was officially terminated on *September 2, 2026*, which is your official divorce date (September 31, 2026, is the date the court entered your judgment into the court system and stamped the documents on the upper right-hand side).
>
> The court also provided certified copies of your judgment, which we requested in the event this is required for the two IRA transfers. We will send each of your certified copies to your current home addresses now and you can initiate both IRA transfers.
>
> At this time, we are just waiting for the court to approve the QDRO for Sam's Gap, Inc. 401(k). As soon as we receive this, we will serve the court-approved

> QDRO to the plan. Once we receive confirmation from the plan that they have received the approved QDRO and will begin their implementation and division of the 401(k), there will be no remaining steps for our office and we will be able to close your file with our office at that time.
>
> Please let us know if you have any questions or if you need any assistance with the IRA transfers. Thank you.

In a case with counsel at the forefront, with clients who prefer not to be on the same email thread, and which includes a private judge engaged to review and approve the judgment and walk the judgment through in a court that can otherwise take six months and still not result in an approved judgment, we might send an email like the following, which includes the court forms known to counsel without any explanations, since this is just to counsel:

> Dear Counsel:
>
> We just received the final approved judgment from Commissioner Mills' office this morning. See below and attached for the filed Judgment, Notice of Entry of Judgment, Declaration for Uncontested Dissolution, Appearance, Stipulations & Waivers, and Stipulation & Waiver of Final Declaration of Disclosure for your files.
>
> I will follow up with separate emails to each of you and your clients with their final approved judgment now. Thank you both.

An example email to both clients with counsel copied might look like this:

> Hi Jen and Matt (and counsel):
>
> We have now received your final approved judgment from the court and have attached the following documents to this email for your records. Please be sure to save these since you will not receive hard copies:
>
> - Final Approved Judgment including the attached Stipulated Judgment.
> - One-page Filed Notice of Entry of Judgment.
> - Filed Judgment Documents (complete file including the above items and related documents required by the court).
> - Confidential Marital Settlement Agreement: Reviewed by the judge and which is not a part of the public court file.
>
> You will see in the box located on the front of the Judgment and Notice of Entry of Judgment that your marital status was officially terminated on January 1, 2026, which is your official divorce date.
>
> Since your case with the court is now complete and we have received confirmation that the agreed equalizing payment has been received, there are no

> remaining steps for our office. We will send our final invoice in the coming weeks and anticipate refunding the remaining unused funds from your trust account. Once we have issued your refunds, we will be able to close your file with our office. Please let us know if you have any questions. Thank you.

Many mediators do not concern themselves with the steps related to concluding the court case. However, in my experience, clients without counsel are not equipped to understand and manage the final case steps and any follow-up required on their own. And in cases with separate counsel, rules of professional responsibility prohibit counsel for one party from communicating directly with another represented party, resulting in inefficiencies and no central management of court requests or other follow-ups, which is often needed at this stage. Because issues of trust, power imbalances, or communication challenges frequently exist in divorce cases, the case managing mediator serves an important role as the neutral case manager, ensuring the case makes it over the finish line for both parties' benefit.

Conclusion: Case Management Matters

Family law mediators often are not aware of the importance of their own role in managing each step of their family law cases. Assuming the role of case managers, mediators are in the ideal position to manage each step in complex family law cases to help our clients achieve their goal of a mediated settlement. And while pro per parties may not always recognize the need for case management at the outset of the case, family law professionals—legal, financial, and mental health professionals alike—understand and typically appreciate the mediator stepping into the often-overlooked role of case manager in family law cases. My hope with this book is that mediators will embrace their case management role and that separate attorneys will encourage greater case management from the mediators in their cases as well.

As mediators, our goals are aligned with the goals of the clients and their separate counsel to help move the case forward to a resolution that meets the needs of both clients without the need for litigation. Case management can bring efficiency and productivity into cases that can easily get bogged down in a labyrinthian process with infinite nuances in the substantive details. Neutral case management increases collaboration and teamwork with other family law professionals for the best possible outcome for the families involved.

For the separate attorneys, if the mediators in your cases have not yet embraced the role of case manager or you believe the case could benefit from more case management, consider asking the mediator for a case management meeting so the team can collaborate to identify next steps, agree on a timeline, and get the mediator's help to move the case forward to final resolution of all issues. After all, we are all working for the same purpose: to help our clients in the best way possible through an already difficult time in their lives.

I believe we owe it to our clients and to ourselves as professionals doing this work every day to support our clients with the best possible process for achieving their goals and helping them reach agreements in a supported process designed to shepherd them efficiently and thoughtfully through their case.

As an eternally optimistic mediator (how else could we do this work?), I hope to inspire other family law professionals to see neutral case management as a powerful tool to bring transparency, efficiency, organization, and collaboration to the complex world of family law cases. I also hope to see more transitions into mediation as a full-time career path and deeper appreciation by the separate attorneys of the benefits a case managing mediator can bring to their cases.

We should all want our clients to be able to move on to the next chapter in their lives knowing they were treated with respect and dignity throughout this process and that we all—as their family law professionals—were instrumental in working together to create that for our shared clients.

Index

About the Author

Paula M. Lawhon is a full-time family law mediator and Family Law Specialist certified by the State Bar of California and has mediated family law cases for more than 20 years at Lawhon Law & Mediation, P.C. She received her Juris Doctor from UC Law San Francisco (formerly UC Hastings) in 1999, graduating as a Public Interest Scholar. She received her Bachelor of Arts from UC Irvine in 1996, graduating *cum laude* and Phi Beta Kappa. Paula is a frequent presenter and author in the field of family law mediation, including integrative mediation models and innovations in dispute resolution and case management. Paula lives and works in the San Francisco Bay Area and enjoys the beautiful weather with her husband, teenage son, and lively Pomeranian.